THE WORKING ACTOR

A No Bullshit Approach to Winning the Acting Game

Pat Skipper

Praise for
The Working Actor

Pat Skipper's *The Working Actor* is a practical, easy-to-follow, sometimes unconventional and often hilarious guide for actors at all levels based on the real-world experiences of a true Hollywood veteran. I've worked with Pat Skipper on both my TV series and the guy delivered on every take. This made him stand out as a go-to guy. His insights on the business and the craft of acting are well earned and invaluable to anyone who wants to become a professional and always working actor.
—Bestselling author & Producer Michael Connelly (*Bosch, The Lincoln Lawyer*)

Excellent, thoughtful and fresh advice. I just kept laughing my ass off. I would absolutely recommend *The Working Actor* not only to those thinking of trying a career in film and TV but to those of us who need to reevaluate our situations, give ourselves a kick in the ass, discover something new or be reminded of what we were doing that was working for us before. It is so much fun to read.
—Kurtwood Smith, (*That '70s Show, Robocop*)

A powerful message to all actors, both novice and veteran alike. This book is a breath of fresh air, written by someone who has walked the walk. It's a healthy (and welcome) dose of 'tough love' and should be a part of every serious actor's library.
—Billy DaMota, CSA (Hollywood Casting Director)

I'm often asked (really, like twice a day) what advice I have for beginning actors. I struggle to put some useful, helpful words together, but I rarely feel as if I've done much good. Pat Skipper has now solved my problem. Anytime anyone asks me what they need to do as a new actor, I'll tell them, "Buy a copy of *The Working Actor* and read the hell out of it!" Nothing I've learned in nearly five decades as an actor is missing from this book, and there's a great deal more in it I wish I'd known all these years. This is a gutsy, funny, straightforward, bawdy, and indispensable book.
—Jim Beaver (*Deadwood, Justified, Supernatural*)

Get off your ass!! Pat Skipper's wonderful book is a feast of useful information and entertaining stories that will help any actor, new or seasoned, be a better actor, and with a little work, a better human being. Do something! Start by reading this book.
—Troy Evans *(Bosch, E.R.)*

Pat Skipper pulls no punches describing acting as a contact sport. *The Working Actor* balances enough cynicism and hope for the beginning actors crazy enough to break into this business, and it's entertaining enough for us survivors that remain. It's as refreshing and exciting as a cold, hard, slap in face; Welcome to show-biz!
—Mark Moses *(Mad Men, Desperate Housewives)*

Doesn't pull any punches. Every young actor should have a read!
—Joel McKinnon Miller *(Brooklyn Nine-Nine, Big Love)*

Copyright © 2015 by Pat Skipper

All rights reserved. This book or any portion thereof may not be reproduced or used in any manner whatsoever without the express written permission of the publisher except for the use of brief quotations in a book review.

Printed in the United States of America
First Printing, 2015

ISBN: 978-0-9965381-1-4

Published By:
Working Actor Media
1125 E Broadway Suite 21
Glendale, CA 91205
www.workingactormedia.com
Email me: workingactormedia@gmail.com

Editor: Josh Galitsky
Cover Design: J.T. Lindroos
Book Design, Formatting: Steven W. Booth, www.GeniusBookServices.com
Author's Photo: David Zaugh

TABLE OF CONTENTS

Foreword ix
Preface xiii
Chapter One: Turning Pro 1
Chapter Two: How Do I Get an Agent? 16
Chapter Three: Death to Art 31
Chapter Four: The Method(s) 48
Chapter Five: Affective Memory 60
Chapter Six: Imagination 79
Chapter Seven: The Behavior of Our Scene Partners 87
Chapter Eight: Improvisation 99
Chapter Nine: Given Circumstances 108
Chapter Ten: What's My Motivation? 125
Chapter Eleven: Making Choices 133
Chapter Twelve: Storytelling 144
Chapter Thirteen: Sports Psychology 158
Chapter Fourteen: Overnight Success 180
Chapter Fifteen: The Commandments of Auditions 192
Chapter Sixteen: Rehearsal 208
Chapter Seventeen: External Interference 217
Chapter Eighteen: Spooky Action at a Distance 226

Acknowledgments 241

Endnotes 245

*"Our life is part folly, part wisdom.
Whoever writes about it only reverently
and according to the rules leaves out
more than half of it."*
—Montaigne

*"I'm a skilled professional actor.
Whether or not I've any talent is
beside the point."*
—Michael Caine

DEDICATED TO

Laura, Matt, Alejandra, Leandro, Fenix, Roy, Samantha, Edward, Tarek, Kelvin, Tessa, Brian, Larvell, Galeit and everyone else in the world who lives to act—and acts to live.

FOREWORD

by Titus Welliver

In 1981, after an uneventful year at Bennington College, I packed an Army duffel and hopped a bus to New York. I enrolled at the HB Studios to study acting.

The tuition was affordable and there were some excellent teachers there. NYC wasn't cheap and I worked several jobs to pay my way. I hadn't had any formal training prior to HB—only some experience doing a few plays in high school and appearing in some films directed by Red Grooms and Rudy Burckhardt. I immersed myself in my studies, snuck in to theatres to see films and plays (I truly couldn't afford the tickets) and just absorbed all that I could.

I got my first paying gig in 1982. St. Marks Poetry Project was doing an adaptation of a Chinese myth, *The White Snake*. I got the male lead. The show opened and did well—the audience a who's-who of the Art and Quality Lit crowd.

I quickly discovered that no agents were talent hunting in the downtown forest of the Avant-Garde. So it goes.

A year later I decided to go back to school to finish my education at NYU. NYU's undergrad program offered students the opportunity to study at several different acting studios (Circle in the Square, Stella Adler, Lee Strasberg and David Mamet's Practical Aesthetics Workshop). I did time at all of the studios.

Bruce Lee studied all the disciplines of combat when conceiving his fighting system, Jeet Kune Do. Worked for Bruce. Worked for me. I think developing an acting technique is like creating a recipe. Try a little of this and a little of that and when it tastes good, that's your soup.

I flourished at NYU and did play after play. I studied with amazing chaps like William Ivey Long and David Mamet. I worked my ass off, kept my head down, realizing that this was my time to learn and, of course, to sometimes fail.

When I graduated, it got quiet. Real quiet. There were no job placement services after leaving the acting conservatory. No agents came to recruit. Crickets were chirping. I hunkered down, did plays for no money, worked jobs to eat and even took the civil servants exam to become a NYC cop. Why not?

In 1986, I was playing Teach in a production of *American Buffalo* directed by the great playwright, Frank Pugliese. The experience was pure joy and it took my game to another level.

Still no agent.

But one evening I was shooting some stick at my go-to saloon when a gentleman approached me.

"Are you Titus Welliver?" Hmmmm? No outstanding warrants. Don't borrow from the shylocks.

"I am."

"I saw you in *American Buffalo* and thought you were great. Who's your agent?" spoke the man.

"Don't have one. Five in the corner," I replied cooly.

The gentleman was in fact a talent agent of excellent reputation. I signed with him the next day. This wasn't a drugstore and I'll remind you I had been kicking around town for a long time. So it goes...

I started booking small roles in feature films and eventually got some attention from the left coast and headed to LA. I refer to this time as the Dog Years.

A year ago, I landed the plum role of Harry Bosch on the Amazon Studios series, *Bosch*. Bosch is a dream role, a man with a strong moral compass—compassionate and tough with a relentless drive to obtain justice for victims of murder. I am very fortunate and my gratitude knows no bounds for this gift of *Bosch*.

In the summer of 2014, Pat Skipper was cast as Sam Delacroix, the father of a murdered boy whose skeletal remains are discovered in the Hollywood Hills after many years. Harry Bosch catches the cold case.

Pat and I had worked together on a film (when we still used film) way back when. We had many mutual friends. We shared an agent. I had seen Pat's work over the years and always thought he was a righteous cat.

I was thrilled that the extremely difficult role of Delacroix was in the hands of an artist such as Pat. He and I would shoot the shit in the makeup trailer—our kids, friends, the business, the piss poor work ethic of some the youngsters we'd had to work with and so on.

Without spoiling it for those who have not seen Pat's work on *Bosch* (watch it, it's a master class), the part is an armload of pain that most actors would be afraid to touch. I really looked forward to shooting those scenes with Pat, despite the profound heaviness of the content, because I got to sit across the table from a real actor, an actor who leapt in to the abyss on every take with complete abandon. It was a privilege. It made me a better actor.

Over the years I have been fortunate to work with many top shelf actors, directors and writers. Very few duds. The consistent work principle I live by is to never get too comfortable. I show up ready to swing, no matter what the role.

When one begins the journey, or shall I say chooses the irresponsible path of becoming an actor, tools for navigation are essential. Yes, there is a long list of required reading, much of which has great merit and some that should have been left inside the writers' heads.

Thankfully, Pat Skipper did not leave this book inside his head. It's a roadmap for every working actor—even for old dogs like me who need an inspiring tap on the shoulder.

And I sure as hell wish I'd had a book like this when I was coming up.

The book is not just pure, tough love for the actor but a record of Pat's road, which had no shortcuts. He tells the whole story, even the ugly parts, to save other actors from some pain.

Read this book! Read it again!

All art is not subjective. There is good art and bad art. Strive to make good art. Show up early, know your lines, listen and be grateful.

So it goes…

Titus Welliver
Hollywood, 2015.

PREFACE

Welcome to the Jungle

"It's fun to be an actor, but as everybody in this room knows, it's a true privilege to be a Working Actor."
—Edward Norton

If plain talk and coarse language offend you, STOP READING NOW. You're probably in the wrong fucking business.

Fair warning: this ain't your Grandpa's acting book.

Most of the acting texts you'll find on the shelves at the Samuel French Bookshop weren't written by actors. They were written by directors and teachers, and in one particularly egregious case, by a famous playwright. The books are dull. Most of the authors are dead.

What I have to offer you is my three decades of experience as a Working Actor.

I have no other job. Hell, I have no other skills. I've gone out on thousands and thousands of auditions. I've won enough jobs to pay my bills.

As a bonus, I'm still very much alive. I'm still auditioning. And I still work as an actor. I, like you, am still "fighting the good fight."

༄

Speaking of dead guys, Robert Lewis was one of the 28 original members of the groundbreaking Group Theatre in the 1930's, along with the most influential acting teachers of the last century: Lee Strasberg, Sanford Meisner and Stella Adler. Lewis co-founded the Actor's Studio in the 1940's, where heavy hitters like Brando, DeNiro and Pacino were nurtured.

Lewis was *also* a very successful Broadway director *(Brigadoon, Witness for the Prosecution, Harold and Maude)* before he headed to the Yale School of Drama to chair the Acting program in the 1970's.

Under the leadership of Lewis and director/producer/critic Robert Brustein, the YSD developed into one of the preeminent acting conservatories in the world. Many Working Actors passed through Lewis' studio, most notably Meryl Streep.

Lewis told the L.A. Times (2/17/1985):

"Every time a young American actor gets up to tackle a classic, one of two things happens. Either he succeeds in getting the inner line right, but he mangles the verse, and Hamlet comes out sounding like Bobby instead of Hamlet ... or, he starts singing and posturing away in what he thinks is the style of the period, and comes out looking like some bad British actor. That's equally bad. Now how do you solve this? By training. Otherwise you have to wait until you have geniuses, and you can't have a theater with geniuses. You need working actors."

THE BUSINESS NEEDS WORKING ACTORS.

It took a long time for me to figure out that I wasn't a genius. (Of course, I was the last to know.)

But what I am is a Working Actor.

I'm just some guy. I grew up in a small Southern town. I'm reasonably smart and tolerably good-looking. I'm kind of tall. I had caring parents who saved their money and sent me to good schools. I studied hard (when it suited me). I've been able to survive on my acting for more than thirty years.

For the purposes of writing *The Working Actor,* I picked out eight young actors, rented a space and, over the next nine months, worked them like pack mules.

In Studio A, we tried out a lot of stuff. Some of it worked. Some of it didn't.

The Working Actor is the result of our explorations in Studio A and my many years of experience on the set and in audition rooms.

The book includes personal anecdotes of events that have influenced my ideas about acting, advice on how best to approach your career as a Working Actor and powerful acting exercises that will help build your Emotional Skill Set.

I don't pull any punches in *The Working Actor*.

Success in this field requires that you develop the mental toughness of a professional athlete while at the same time retaining your humanity. The first few chapters specifically deal with this approach.

If I come off as blunt at times, I offer no apology. Think of me as your loving yet brutally honest coach.

The middle chapters of *The Working Actor* will show you how to bring *life* to your work by using my particular approach to the techniques handed down to us by our elders: the great actors and teachers who preceded us.

I also explore sports psychology, and I will teach you how to decrease the nervousness that gets in the way of your success.

Finally, I attack auditions.

You can't be a Working Actor if you can't win jobs.

To help you increase your odds of winning, I offer you my "Fifteen Commandments"—the dos and don'ts of auditioning. Based on my decades of experience "in the room," it's practical advice that'll GET YOU WORK.

You can't learn how to act from a book anymore than you can learn how to hit home runs by skimming the Sports section. The only way to learn how to act is to GET UP AND ACT.

However, you can certainly be nudged into reexamining your approach. You can find things to try out. You will, I hope, find inspiration from the victories [copious defeats] of the author.

If there's something you can use in this book, by all means use it. If not, chuck it and move on. No harm, no foul.

CHAPTER ONE

Turning Pro

*"When the going gets weird,
the weird turn pro."*
—Hunter S. Thompson

The business needs Working Actors. It's your job to turn yourself into one.

A few years back, I took an old high school friend and her sixteen-year-old daughter to lunch at the Disney Commissary. (By the way, "commissary" is glamorous movie-speak for "cafeteria.") The daughter was a beautiful kid with a boatload of talent. As I recall, we passed a pleasant hour mulling over her career possibilities.

Later, I spoke to my friend who relayed that her daughter was "disappointed." I couldn't figure out what she was talking about. Did the food suck? No, indeed. Apparently, the child was upset because she hadn't been "discovered" while she was wolfing down her cheeseburger. I was, to say the least, flabbergasted.

Look, the biggest con job ever perpetrated by Hollywood marketing execs is the self-serving mythology of "overnight success." Ever since the studios pumped up the legend of Lana Turner being "discovered" while drinking a milkshake at Schwab's Pharmacy in the 1930s, wide-eyed suckers from Anchorage to Zip City have descended upon Tinseltown in endless droves, expecting to run into a mogul who is passing out movie roles at the bus station.

I hate to break it to you, but there are no "talent scouts" out there looking for you.

The chances of someone discovering you in L.A. while you sip anything anyplace are roughly the same as the manager asking you to pitch at Dodger Stadium because he liked the way you nibbled your hot dog while you sat in the stands.

How many baseball players make it to "The Bigs" without busting ass? The answer is: exactly none.

Everyone in the world intrinsically understands this. Everybody knows that these guys lift weights to the point of exhaustion, work tirelessly on their Fundamentals, hit thousands of balls in the cage, run endless numbers of wind sprints and execute countless fielding drills.

Ballplayers reach the top by *increasing their athletic potential* through hard work. No one gives them anything. They earn it.

The same holds true for actors.

There are no shortcuts. If you want to have a career as a Working Actor, I'm here to tell you that the only "Performance Enhancing Drug" is for you to get out there and bust your ass every single day.

☙

Increase your odds of winning. Change your approach.

I once caught a dress rehearsal of a college production of Sophocles' *Oedipus Rex*. The evening was memorable for three reasons:

First, the men wore leather loincloths and their chests were oiled up like baby butts. I was glad to only be in the audience and not on stage.

Second, thanks no doubt to some "crackerjack" university dramaturgy, they pronounced Oedipus so that it sounded (at least to my semi-stoned, sophomoric ears) like they were saying "EAT-a-puss." (Needless to say, I had tremendous difficulty keeping a straight face the whole night.)

And third, the director made a very illuminating comment while giving notes after the run-through—proving that if you keep your ears open, you can learn from anyone.

"Actors are athletes," he said. "Not sexual athletes. Not booze athletes. Not dope athletes. Actors are *theatre* athletes. This is a difficult show. Rest up. Take care of your bodies."

Having just endured hours of oily, leathery puss eating, it occurred to me that the sex, drugs and rock 'n' roll athletes on that stage outnumbered the theatre athletes by a ratio of about 40 to zero. Nonetheless, the guy did have a point.

Actors are athletes.

Oedipus is a brutally difficult undertaking for any group of actors. The physical demands are as extreme as any sport you can name. No doubt every linebacker in the country would vehemently disagree, but throw one of them into Oedipus' chorus and there's a decent chance that he'd be an embarrassed, burned-out, laryngitis victim before the show ever hit previews.

☙

Quit thinking of yourself as an Artist. You're a Professional Athlete.

The most accurate paradigm for a career in the "Acting Game" is Major League Baseball.

Actors and athletes are paid to deliver on cue. "Artists"—painters and sculptors—work when the inspiration hits them. They can take a nap or work until dawn. They can go to dinner or cruise the net for porn. Their art is finished when they say it's finished. It can take months or even years for them to complete a project.

Meanwhile, actors act when the director calls, "Action." Actors finish acting when the director says, "Cut." Baseball players play when the man in blue yells, "Play ball!" They play until someone wins.

Baseball is a team sport. A single player, no matter how great he is, can't do squat without a team.

Acting is a team sport, too. With the exception of the occasional star-driven, one-man show, the Working Actor needs somebody to act with—usually a whole bunch of somebodies to act with.

As in baseball, acting rewards individual achievement.

In baseball, the big hitter and the ace pitcher get all the attention (and the monster paychecks) but over the long season, they can't win without strong, everyday teammates backing them up. Even the utility catcher and the pinch hitter often play critical roles during a pennant run.

In a good film, the star may win the awards and grab almost all the cash, but she still needs solid Working Actors in order to succeed.

Finding work on a Major League Baseball team is a bitch. Each roster holds twenty-five men. There are thirty teams.

Even taking into account the forty-man roster (which includes injured players and some minor leaguers who only come up for a quick cup of coffee) there are only 1,200 total jobs that can be had if you plan to make your living working as a Big Leaguer. Every year, 130,000 baseball athletes graduate from high school. Do the math.

While there are more jobs in total to be had in the Acting Game, the chances of making a living are equally as miniscule.

There are over 150,000 members of SAG-AFTRA.

In 2012 alone, approximately 18,000 of the members earned above the paltry $16,000 threshold required to qualify for basic health insurance benefits. A fraction of those 18,000 Working Actors will make enough to survive on without also having a day job.

The commercial similarities between acting and baseball diverge at this point, as the *minimum* salary for a 2013 ballplayer was $490,000. If you were lucky enough to make your insurance in SAG, you're a winner! (Dirt poor perhaps, but a winner.)

Very few screen actors, even the working ones, are making any real money. The *average* MLB salary is 3.2 million bucks. If you're pulling down that kind of dough as an actor, congratulations! You're a star! Put this book down right now and go for a latte!

The saving grace for Working Actors over ballplayers is that some actors are good enough to work until they're old and decrepit. Baseball players break down when they're still young. At that point, of course, some of them try to take up acting.

There's an old joke. A young actor is walking off the stage during a performance. An old actor asks:

"What did you do with the money, honey?"

"What money?" asks the young actor.

"The money your Momma gave you for your acting lessons."

The Acting Game doesn't have a paid Minor League system like baseball. "Minor League" actors work for free in plays and student films and in whatever else they can find. Unlike ballplayers, they don't pick up a check for learning The Game. Actors *pay* to go to class.

By default, the conservatories, colleges and universities have become the Minor Leagues of the Acting Game.

There are now over 200 U.S. schools that crank out BA or BFA degrees in Acting. That's about 10,000 newly-minted actors every year, not to mention all the MFA graduates rolling off the assembly line. And that doesn't include the thousands of kids who skip college and plunge right into the business.

Every cute kid who has ever gotten high on the addictive buzz of applause and acclaim in the school play has at least entertained the notion of becoming a "movie star." The Acting Game is pretty much crammed with the prettiest girl and hardest-abbed boy from every small town U.S. of A. production of *Grease*.

Every year, approximately 18,000 *new* actors try to enter a field that boasts only 18,000 *total* positions.

☙

Back when I was first starting out (when dinosaurs still roamed around the La Brea Tar Pits), I had precisely one friend who was "making it." The guy was a director who routinely got jobs directing the classics on college campuses all around the country. He was on staff at The Juilliard School. To me, the dude was a superstar.

But even with his success, he later decided to switch careers because, in part, he felt that preparing kids for a business that neither wanted nor needed them was, in his words, "immoral."

Here's a nasty little secret:

The majority of these acting schools suck. It's quite possible to graduate from some of these programs in serious debt and end up being a worse actor than when you started.

I attended two of the better schools in the country. Florida State and Yale both had top programs. Yet, neither of these schools had a systematic, coherent approach to acting at that time. Some of the teachers were great. Others weren't. It was a total crapshoot.

Both schools offered adequate teaching in the Fundamentals: voice, speech, movement, etc., but when it came to the instruction of acting, it was a real mixed bag. If the teacher knew what he or she was doing, you could learn something. If not, you were lucky if you didn't come out at the other end a quivering mess of confusion and self-doubt.

And these were the *good* schools!

I was fortunate to have sat in the classrooms of some very committed, competent and caring teachers in my day.

However, among the 200+ schools in the Theatre diploma business, there are a lot of students who are getting next to nothing for their money. These schools are in the business of staying in business. These programs take on nearly all comers, regardless of the students' abilities, so long as these kids are keeping the electric bill paid and the salary checks coming.

☙

So now that I have depressed you with the cold, hard facts about the Acting Game, you're probably thinking to yourself, "Why am I reading this fucking book? I've heard all this before. I get it. It's a tough road. Have a back-up plan. Yada yada yada. This guy is bumming me out."

Sorry. That's not my intention at all.

I know that people in your life have tried to discourage you from the get-go. They may have even quoted some of these demoralizing stats.

They've said stupid shit like, "Who the hell do you think you are? It's a fantasy. Get a real job."

My parents weren't exactly thrilled with the concept either. My dad had delusions of me becoming his attorney. (Poor bastard.)

However, to their credit, my parents eventually came around to the idea and became very supportive. I finally got them to see how much I wanted it and how hard I was willing to work for it. (Getting accepted into a school with a fancy, Ivy League name didn't hurt my cause either.)

Personally, when it comes to the Acting Game, I never dissuade anyone from giving it a try. What's the worst thing that can happen? You fail. So what?

Theodore Roosevelt once famously said:

"Far better is it to dare mighty things, to win glorious triumphs, even though checkered by failure ... than to rank with those poor spirits who neither enjoy nor suffer much, because they live in a gray twilight that knows not victory nor defeat."

I have lots of friends who went the conventional route. They followed the rules. They made their parents proud. They went to law school. They graduated—and quickly discovered that they *hated* practicing law.

One buddy of mine went all the way through med school and residency before he finally stood up for himself and got back into acting.

Don't be that guy.

Even if you fail (and sorry, but the numbers suggest that you will) you'll be a healthier and happier person for having taken a chance on yourself.

And you'll never have to regret not trying. That I can guarantee.

Believe me, I'm not laying all these stats on you in order to steer you away from the Acting Game. I'm on your side.

But I do think it's imperative that you understand what you're up against so that you can begin to formulate a winning approach.

First of all, you've got to know what game you're playing.

When I went to Yale Drama School, the mission statement was (and I'm paraphrasing here) to "prepare students to work in the Regional Repertory Theatre." It was complete bullshit!

The Regional Theatre "experiment" was already failing by the 1980s. Already gone were most of the companies that would hire groups of actors for an entire season to play multiple roles in multiple plays.

Gone too were those wonderful nine months' worth of paychecks. Right down the street from me at the Yale Rep, actors were ferried up by train from New York to do a single show for a couple of months and were then cut loose.

The "mission" of my school was to give false hope to its students about their "artistic" futures; to prepare its graduates for careers that did not exist and to train its "Theatre Athletes" for a game that no one was playing.

Here's a fucking mission statement for you:

I'm turning pro and I'm going to win.

ଏଓ

How are you going to win?

Well, we've got seventeen more chapters to work that out, but the fact that you haven't tossed this book in the trash and gone running off to play around on Facebook (after I've been so rough on you) shows that you aren't easily discouraged. Good.

This is a war of attrition. *Resiliency* is right up there with "talent" on the scale of important traits you've got to have in order to win at this Game.

You're beginning to understand though that, like the lottery, the odds are stacked heavily against you.

For example, how many athletes do you know personally who've made the transition from your college (or high school) to pro sports? For most of you, the likely answer is none. Probably no one you've ever met in your entire life has had the "right stuff."

Obviously, Working Actors, like professional athletes, need to have ability. It's probably not going to matter how hard you work if you're simply not good enough. I can't help you there. Nobody can.

Hell, most baseball players die on the vine in high school or college. The rest get weeded out in the Minors. This is true for actors, too.

Playing Tony in *West Side Story* at Anthony D. Weiner High School or Shakespeare's Juliet at Boll Weevil State College of the Arts doesn't mean squat in the professional world. The awful truth is that ninety-five percent of those fresh-faced, BFA-holding, would-be "actors" will be out of the game in five years or less. After that, maybe a mere handful will stick.

The good news is that some people will make it. Why not you?

જી

I know this kid who used to live in the country club community of Isleworth, Florida near Windermere. He had a neighbor by the name of Tiger Woods. Perhaps you've heard of him.

Anyway, the kid was a pretty good high school golfer. Every day after school, he'd drop off his books and head to the club. When he would arrive, Tiger would be in the process of hitting range balls with his coach.

This kid would hit a large bucket of seventy-five balls, and then he'd run out for 18 practice holes on the course. When the kid would return several hours later, Tiger Woods would still be standing on the range, hitting balls with his coach.

At the time the kid told me this story, Tiger Woods was at the top of his form and was dominating the world of golf. He was also an international celebrity.

And what was Tiger doing on his day off?

He was sweating his ass off in the stifling Florida humidity, spanking golf balls with a coach.

Tiger Woods is a once-in-a-generation phenomenon. He is inarguably one of the greatest sportsmen in the history of the world, and he certainly has the world's best work ethic.

For all I know, you may very well be the next Tiger Woods of the Acting Game. If so, who are you to kick back and hang out, waiting to be discovered? Get the hell out there and hit some practice balls!

For the rest of us "less-than-genius" actors, we need to work *doubly* hard.

As former Notre Dame football coach Lou Holtz once said, "No one has ever drowned in sweat."

~

Early in its run, I landed a great part on the TV show, *Bones*.

Temperance Brennan, the lead character played by Emily Deschanel, is a forensic pathologist. Every week, they bring her a dead guy, and she does a bunch of TV Hocus Pocus and solves the crime.

In this one episode, the dead "guy" turns out to be Brennan's own mother who has been missing for decades. The clues all point to me. I'm a hitman who's in witness protection and I'm posing as, of all things, a pig farmer. (Fucking TV. Makes no sense.)

Although the concept was ludicrous, it was a surprisingly well-written part, and I was very proud of the way it turned out. The check cashed. Nice residuals, too.

Deschanel's co-star on *Bones* is David Boreanaz who plays Seeley Booth, a rough-around-the-edges, FBI Special Agent who helps her track down the baddies. (It *really* makes no sense at all.) However, this guy Boreanaz really impressed me.

Now, David Boreanaz isn't exactly the Tiger Woods of Acting. He's no genius. Far from it. He cuts a handsome and confident male presence onscreen that audiences find appealing. And he's a solid actor.

But Boreanaz understands what sells TV shows like this—the relationship between the main characters.

In the scenes I had with them, Boreanaz constantly worked between takes with Deschanel, searching for ways to enhance their onscreen chemistry. He labored to massage the moments, probing for nuances.

During the shots, he kept changing things up, striving to make every take as fresh and spontaneous as he possibly could.

Later, an actress who knows David Boreanaz told me that he meets with a coach every Sunday, and together they comb through the next week's script looking for ways for David to bring some *life* to his material.

Believe me, not everyone on TV is working as hard as this guy.

Playing the lead in an hour-long drama is exhausting. It takes about nine months to shoot a 24-episode season. The hours are crushing.

Every Monday morning you're in the makeup chair before the sun comes up and you don't finish until after dark on Friday, with 12-hour days (at minimum) sandwiched in between. Most TV folks aren't working this hard on their Sundays off (and if you watch much, you can tell.)

What does Boreanaz get for all the effort he puts in?

He's one of the highest paid actors on TV. He's got a big old house and a Playmate wife.

More importantly, Boreanaz gets scripts delivered to his door every week. He's gotten almost a decade's worth of acting work out of it. He has negotiated a producer credit, and he gets to direct. Not a bad deal for a working stiff.

Once upon a time, David Boreanaz was just a Working Actor who went on an audition for some random pilot called *Bones*. You get my drift?

You don't have to be God's gift to acting to become a star.

In baseball, a Hall of Fame hitter is just a good hitter who keeps on getting hits. A star is just a Working Actor who keeps on working, keeps getting better and then keeps on working some more.

Here are a few quick tips:

- If you're not in class, get in class.

- If you don't have an audition coach, get an audition coach. Tiger Woods has a coach. David Boreanaz has a coach.

- Practice every single day. That's what Woods and Boreanaz do. Al Pacino still puts up scenes at The Actors Studio, and he's Al Fucking Pacino. The man is in his 70s for Chrissake.

***Think of yourself as an Athlete. Develop a Work Ethic.
Work on your Fundamentals. Develop your Skill Set.***

You *just never know* when it'll be your turn to enter the Acting Game.

MAKE DAMN SURE YOU'RE READY TO WIN IT.

CHAPTER TWO

How Do I Get an Agent?

*"I wish to be cremated.
One tenth of my ashes shall be given
to my agent, as written in our contract."*
—Groucho Marx

Chapter Two used to be Chapter Eighteen, because in terms of importance, getting an agent should be way down the priority list for actors who have limited experience. But I'm sure that you, like most actors, probably think otherwise.

For instance, as a favor for a friend, I took a meeting with this kid who had graduated college with a business degree and was working at a civilian job. Bored to tears, he stumbled upon a weekend acting class.

"I really liked it," he said, his eyes glistening as if he were stoned.

After a grand total of 12 lessons, he quit his job and moved to Hollywood to turn pro. As far as I could ascertain, he'd never even been in the school play. The very first question he asked me during our meeting was:

"How do I get an agent?"

I've got to admit, I sort of admired the kid's chutzpah, but WTF was he thinking?

But he's not the only one putting the cart before the horse. I've spoken to groups of college acting students and have been in acting classes with young actors, and time and time again, the first (and sometimes only) question that they'll ask is, "How do I get an agent?"

Look, it's not a *stupid* question. In fact, it's a very good question but it's the *wrong* question at this stage of the game.

But knowing that you probably would skip ahead to Chapter Eighteen anyway (I know *I* would have!), I moved the discussion up here to Chapter Two to give you the real scoop on getting an agent. No need to thank me.

Drama Schools certainly can't teach their students what's what with agents. The vast majority of college instructors have probably never even *met* an agent, much less *had* an agent.

Once again, that leaves you the actor stuck out there on your lonesome. Having been down this rough patch of agent road a few times, let me be your tour guide.

☙

First of all, let's talk about what agents do:

Agents submit us for projects. Agents set up the appointments for our auditions. Agents field our offers over the phone and Internet. They negotiate our deals. They call us with the good news. They thank us for the flowers we send them. And they take a 10% commission off the top of our paychecks.

Secondly, let's talk about what agents don't do:

Agents DO NOT get us work.

Let me repeat that. Agents DO NOT get us work.

You know who *does* get us work? *We* get us work.

This is an incredibly important lesson that even some of the most hardened veteran actors never learn. I cannot tell you how many conversations I've been privy to that go something like the following short movie:

CRAZY ASS BRUCE

(A Spike Lee Joint)

ACTOR #1 (portrayed by me) goes to some play because he's got a friend in the cast and can't fucking get out of it.

At intermission, ACTOR #1 is approached by ACTOR #2 (portrayed by Bruce Willis), a guy ACTOR #1 may have worked with for half a day about 8 years ago or perhaps with whom ACTOR #1 was vaguely acquainted when they were both clients at the same agency way back in the day.

(As far as I know, Mr. Willis was never in this position but my hypothetical friend, Spike, insisted we needed a star name in our imaginary blockbuster movie.)

BRUCE WILLIS (sweat glistening off his bald noggin): Hey! How's it goin'? Haven't seen you in, like, forever. Who's your agent now?

ME: I'm with Associated Clownsticks.

BRUCE WILLIS: Yeah? Yeah? I hear they're good. Are they good?

ME (cagily, knowing what's coming): I've had worse.

BRUCE WILLIS: Man, could you put in a word? These guys I'm with, I just don't get it. I got four auditions last year. Four! And I fucking nailed two of them! That's a 50% booking rate. With a track record like that, you'd think they'd be busting their asses trying to get me out there. I'm a booking machine, man!

CUT TO: Having extricated himself, ACTOR #1 (me) collapses into his theater seat, furiously brushing at his sleeves in a hopeless attempt to remove the desperate *Loser Dust*.

༄

Look, here's the deal:

Actors are shoes. Agents are shoe salesmen who work on commission.

What Bruce can't quite glom on to is that strappy sandals are in this season and he's a clog. He's last month's flavor. He is out-of-style.

Now look, there's nothing in the world that Bruce's agents would like more than for their crazy ass client to get more auditions.

First of all, he may actually make them a little coin.

Secondly, he might quit bugging them all the time—and Bruce is the type who calls, sends emails, drops by (oy, does he drop by!) and generally makes a greasy nuisance of himself on a day-to-day basis.

You see, the problem is that nobody wants to see poor old Crazy Ass Bruce right now.

Casting Directors aren't calling to request his cheesy presence at auditions. When his agents try to sell him, they're greeted with a polite silence or a "Who else have you got?" Eventually, Bruce's agents simply stop pushing.

Switching over to Associated Clownsticks (or any other talent agency for that matter) isn't going to change the fact that Bruce is yesterday's news. And these agencies aren't going to be interested in him anyway because Bruce doesn't have anything they can sell, either.

Bruce doesn't know he's passé. But he'd better figure it out quickly or his career is going to *Die Hard*.

☙

Being an actor's agent is not an easy job. There's tons of competition for that precious 10% and scaring up appointments for clients is hard work.

Bringing on a new client, particularly one without any professional experience, is tough sledding for an agent.

Getting auditions for a young actor with minimal credits means the agent has to bust her ass. She's got to vouch for and sell that actor hard, putting her reputation on the line.

Agents are not thrilled to risk burning their cred with the casting community for little or no return. If her new client "pokes the pup" at the audition (as newbie actors are prone to do) getting him a second chance will require a Herculean effort.

And frankly, many agents just don't care to work that hard.

But, here's the *good* news:

People get signed to agencies all the time. Agents need us actors as much as we need them. We are their meal ticket.

Some of the 10,000 new BFA actors that will graduate next May will get agents. A few of those actors will go on to have great careers.

It might as well be you.

Newness, freshness—youth—are very valuable commodities in the Acting Game. That's what YOU bring to the table. Combine those essential qualities with knowing what the fuck you're doing, and an agent will have a product that they can sell. YOU!

෴

THE PARABLE OF THE PIXIE

I may have been the worst auditioner in the history of the Acting Game when I first started out. Hoping to learn how not to suck, I took a class from a New York Casting Director.

I can't remember who taught this particular workshop or what was discussed, so it's safe to say I didn't learn much from the Casting Director himself.

However, hidden amongst the drossy hoard of would-be actors, was this irrepressible, effervescent pixie of a girl.

She wore her raven hair in a short bob, and her eyes shone with the gleaming possibility of youth. (Seems her Dad's dentist's friend was a producer, and Dr. Overbite had somehow skeeved her an audition for a Broadway show.)

When the pixie told us this tale, a collective eye roll rippled across the surface of the snooty sea of more "in-the-know" actors. Her accent was strictly bridge-and-tunnel. A real Jersey girl.

"Hey," she beamed. "You nevah know!"

As we exited the studio, a pal of mine, curly-haired and bespectacled, turned to me with his best T-Neck accent and ejaculated: "You nevah know!"

"And you know what?" he continued. "She's right! That's the best thing about being an actor!"

I had never seen that delightful little imp from the casting seminar before, and I never saw her again. But she taught me two valuable lessons:

One, if you keep your ears open and your guard down, you can learn from just about anyone.

And secondly, one of the greatest things about acting professionally is that ...

YOU NEVER KNOW!

Most people's adult lives are defined by day-to-day sameness. They know, accounting for some minor variations and barring catastrophe, what's going to happen for the foreseeable future. They show up, put in their time and take home a paycheck. Weekend: rinse and repeat. Think Bill Murray in *Groundhog Day*.

But this is not true of the Working Actor.

One audition, one phone call can spin the Working Actor's life completely off its axis, ejecting her from whatever stale ordinariness or life of quiet desperation she's currently enduring into some completely unexpected, unpredictable and even spectacular new orbit.

That forgettable casting person may have made off with a little bit of my money, but in the end I got what I came for. And I got it from an audacious, unpretentious little sprite.

As the scholarly St. Augustine wrote:

"Do not despair. One of the thieves was saved. Do not presume. One of the thieves was damned." (Sadly, in the movie version of this proverb, the part of Jesus is already cast. Tom Cruise, naturally. And no, Bruce, you can't get a reading for it.)

Essentially, what good old Augustine is saying is, *"You nevah know!"*

⁕

I couldn't get any traction at all when I landed in New York City fresh out of Yale. That was because I sucked. I choked auditions left and right. Moreover, I was like Crazy Ass Bruce. I reeked of desperation. I was going nowhere. Fast!

There was only one viable solution I could come up with: I had to get off my ass and stop sucking.

So, I put myself back into acting class.

I also started doing unpaid readings of new plays around town and got to know a fair number of the cool, young playwrights like [present-day] TV writers Eric Overmeyer *(Bosch, The Wire, Treme)* and James Yoshimura *(Homicide: Life on the Street, Homeland)* and, most consequentially, Alan Bowne *(Beirut, Forty-Deuce).*

I also got to act with younger (and thinner) versions of Kevin Spacey, Laurence Fishburne and Kelsey Grammer. (I can report that all of them actually had hair at one juncture in their lives.)

None of this ever led directly to an acting gig. But what about indirectly?

You never know.

☙

Next thing I realized was:

I need to create my own work. If no one is going to hire me, fuck 'em! I'll hire myself!

I had done a few readings for a group called MCC Theater, founded by Broadway actor and soap star, Bobby LuPone, and a handful of his students at NYU, including Bernie Telsey.

I started hanging around the MCC office, doing this and that, until I might as well have been part of the furniture. One day, Bernie referred to me as a "company member," and that was that.

You never know.

Of course, MCC Theater later became a big deal in New York, home for such names as Philip Seymour Hoffman, Lynn Redgrave, Liev Schreiber and Sigourney Weaver.

The company has won numerous Tonys, Obies, Drama Desk Circle awards, Theater World awards and even a Pulitzer. They've also premiered playwright-in-residence Neil LaBute's plays for at least a decade.

However, at that time, MCC was nothing but a bite-sized nothing burger. The company was mostly known for staging readings of new plays and quixotically foraging for financial backers.

I partnered up with a bow-tie-wearing Southern boy named Will Cantler. What MCC Theater really needed, we figured, was a more public face. And what better way to create a bunch of opportunities than a one-act festival?

Now don't get me wrong, most one-act festivals suck. The writing is uneven, the directing hit-or-miss and the acting is usually all over the map. Most of the folks in the audience are friends and family, and you have to paper the house with freebies to fill it up.

Of course, *our* one-act festival was going to be better than that. Much better.

But … mostly it wasn't.

But you never know.

A year prior, I had done a couple of readings of a play called *The Able-Bodied Seaman* for that shaggy, scrawny and squirrely-looking playwright, Alan Bowne.

Alan was the least healthy-looking dude I had ever met. He smoked and drank and was addicted to smack. However, under his steely armor of cynicism lurked the heart of a true Romantic.

And. The Man. Could. Write.

I clearly recall sitting at my desk (an old door astride a pair of battered filing cabinets) digging through a lamentable mountain of mediocre submissions and finding Alan's name on a cover page. It read:

"*Beirut by Alan Bowne.*"

Thirty minutes later, I sat ecstatic. Blown away. Thunderstruck.

You never know.

So, what happened, you ask?

Cutting to the chase, a [love letter] review by Walter Goodman in *The New York Times* happened. Then, the *New York Post*'s Mel Gussow called for the play to immediately move Off-Broadway.

We were a hit!

Investors parachuted in from all directions. (Obviously, hiring the amazing, then 21-year-old Marisa Tomei to play the lead kinda, sorta helped our cause.)

Beirut ran successfully at the Westside Arts Theater, opened to sold-out houses in L.A. at the Matrix and won a fistful of awards. HBO made an unforgivably crappy movie called *Daybreak* out of it.

You never know.

In the midst of all the insanity of getting the one-act festival off the ground, I landed a tiny fucking part in Oliver Stone's *Wall Street*.

My acting was as stiff as a 3-day-old cadaver, and Oliver wasn't particularly nice to me.

Significantly unimpressed by my first foray into film (but enjoying my newly-minted status as a 28-year-old theatre wunderkind, one-act impresario and dashingly handsome "genius"), I decided to quit acting.

But Bernie Telsey talked me into taking the GUARD role in the L.A. production of *Beirut*.

Although it's an interesting part, the audience never sees the actor's face. It's certainly not a role upon which to build a career. But …

You never know.

The run was a smashing success.

But nothing had really panned out for me personally in L.A., so I was finished with acting. But then …

"Hey, Paaaat," a voice bellowed as I left the theater one cold, Wednesday night.

I turned to find the tall, barrel-chested, New York Italian agent, Joey Comb-Over, silhouetted dramatically under a streetlight.

"Hey, I caught you in *Wall Street*. You looked great onscreen. I'm opening a new L.A. office. You got representation?"

Bada bing, bada boom! A few months later, I found myself in Europe shooting a TV pilot. I've been a Working Actor ever since.

You just never know.

☙

So, back to the original question: *How do I get an agent?*

1. Study your ass off.
2. Vigorously suck for several years.
3. Haul your ass back to acting class.
4. Do a bunch of play readings and worm your way into a theatre company.
5. Produce an underwhelming one-act festival but create a monster hit.
6. Have a crappy experience on a movie set.
7. Almost quit the biz.
8. Move 3000 miles away from home.
9. Play a flyspeck, five-minute stage part in pitch black.
10. Run into a paisan with *really* bad hair.

That's how you get an agent!

Well, that's *my* story, anyway. But the point is: there's not a one-size-fits-all answer to this question.

Some actors meet their agents through a friend or casting person. Some get seen in a play or student film. Some actors catch a break because of a photo. Some actors get signed because their dad's dentist's friend is a Broadway producer.

Most actors, like yours truly, just keep plugging along until "coincidence" smiles upon them.

You just never know.

☙

Want an agent to be motivated to sell you?

Do Your Part. Up Your Game.

Be an *athlete*. Whether you're a young kid or seasoned vet, stay sharp. Don't suck. Work on your acting. Work on it all the time.

Every day. Observe people. Go to class. Go to movies. Go to plays. Work out. Go out and party. Fuck a lot. Get some life experience.

Then, work even harder on your acting.

Say "YES" to everything.

If someone asks you to do a reading of some shitty play, do it. If a student wants you to read for his idiotic film, read for it. If you hear about a bullshit workshop, sign up. If you get invited to a screening or a party, go. No part is too small. Take what you're offered. Work breeds more work.

Do something about your acting career every single day.

Make a phone call. Go to the gym. Read plays. Read literature. Work on a monologue. Watch at least one episode of every show in Primetime. Pick an actress you admire and study every single one of her movies. Send a letter to a director you like. Get a cool haircut. Skip the brownies for a day.

Do *something* every damn day of the week.

Create your own work.

Don't hang around waiting for the phone to ring. Produce a play. Make a video for YouTube. Invite a few friends over and read plays together. Do a web series. Shit, do a puppet show.

Get off your ass. Make it happen. You don't need someone to hire you in order to be a Working Actor. Hire yourself!

Transform yourself.

Turn yourself into the sexiest, shiniest, most happening, kick-ass pair of kinky boots that you possibly can. And then go "all in." Put yourself out there and make the "shoe salespeople" find you. Because when they do, you'll be fucking irresistible.

If you do the work, the agents will come to you.

Give them something to sell. Make them hungry for you. Make them horny for you. Make them greedy for you. Make them afraid to say, "no."

Make THEM desperate for YOU!

That's how you get an agent.

CHAPTER THREE

Death to Art

"All art is quite useless."
—Oscar Wilde

Describing the daunting task he faced performing *Waiting for Godot* on the New York stage, the late Robin Williams said, "I dread the word 'art.' That's what we used to do every night before we'd go on ... we'd go, *'No art. Art dies tonight.'* We'd try to give it a life, instead of making *Godot* so serious."

I agree with Mr. Williams.

Death to Art. Yes to Life.

ை

I got to know a young actor in class once. This kid was very anxious to get ahead. He could act some. He was fairly attractive.

Guys have succeeded with less. But it wasn't happening—at least not quickly enough to satisfy him. The dude was getting desperate—Crazy Ass Bruce desperate.

Let me tell you, there is nothing more unattractive to agents and casting people than a desperate actor. They can smell one coming a mile away.

Look, every single actor that shows up at the audition *really, really, really* wants the job. If we take a meeting with an agent, they *know* that we want them to sign us. Wanting it a *whole, whole* lot doesn't count for shit.

In fact, it can work against us.

Agent meetings and auditions are power situations. Yes, these people have the power to sign us to their agency or hire us for that TV pilot. That's a given.

However, the actor has power in this transaction, too. Agents and Casting Directors need Working Actors in order to survive.

As Working Actors, it is vital that we learn how to sustain our power under these circumstances. Walking into these rooms and turning belly-up like lovesick puppies is a losing proposition.

When we get around to discussing the ins and outs of auditioning, *Maintaining Your Power* will be a major theme. (I'll go on and on and on and on and on about it. I apologize in advance.)

I suggested to this desperate kid (who will henceforth be known as "Bruce the Younger") that maybe he ought to consider putting in some time as a volunteer for a charity.

I encouraged him to get out of his apartment, turn his attention away from himself and towards others who might need it. I thought that it might help him put a few things into perspective. His response was very telling.

"I always thought I'd do that with my acting," said Bruce the Younger. "You know, benefit mankind."

Well, Christ on a riding mower. No wonder Bruce the Younger felt so desperate. Talk about setting yourself up for failure.

Acting, if you haven't noticed, ain't the fucking priesthood. It's not a calling. Your acting isn't going to change the world. It's a great game and it provides opportunities for tremendous athletic highs.

Mainly though, it's a cool way to make a buck.

Like my pal Bruce the Younger, I was something of an asshole when I was starting out. I was very full of myself. (The more things change, the more they remain the same!)

We were a few weeks into filming that pilot I shot in Europe—a TV show based on the World War II movie, *The Dirty Dozen*. We were running way behind.

Exasperated, the British director yelled out: "Let's make this piece of shit!"

I was offended to the bone.

It was my first great job, and I was really into it. "Piece of shit? How dare he! I'm a fucking Artist!"

If you're reading this, you're most likely an acting student. Just as likely, you think of yourself as an Artist just like I did. An Artist, with a capital "A."

Let me tell you, I *get* that. It's okay. A good number of us end up acting because we're a little different than your run-of-the-mill kid, and the Theatre welcomes outcasts from the "Island of Misfit Toys" like us with open arms.

Theatre is a safe haven from the conventional-thinking hacks (cleverly disguised as our contemporaries).

Theatre is a refuge from disapproving parents who only want what's best for us (but do everything they can to break our Spirit).

Theatre is a sanctuary from teachers who are too busy or burnt out to even attempt to inspire us.

Theatre is a shelter from a conformist society that would rather we stay in our little boxes with the lids tightly secured.

Theatre is the place where it's cool to be "out there," or "weird" or "gay" or "wild" or "all of the above."

You're actually *supposed* to be all those things (and more) because you're in the *Theatre*. You're a *Theatre* person. You can be whatever the hell you want to be, probably for the first time in your life.

"I'm not really a freak, after all! I'm an Artist! How awesome is that?"

At the risk of offending you though, you're not an Artist. Artists make art. Actors don't.

☙

What is the work of the Working Actor?

First of all, let's demystify what it is that Working Actors actually do.

I hate to break it to you, but the whole glamour myth of Hollywood life is hokum—a big fat lie.

Movie sets are completely industrial—a collection of "glamorous" semi trucks and "glamorous" hairy dudes whose job it is to carry "glamorous" movie crap around. Lunch comes out of a "glamorous" roach coach and is served on "glamorous" folding tables.

Get the picture?

Aside from the mountains of money and armies of annoying strangers that want to have sex with them ...

What do stars have that other Working Actors don't?

Big trailers.

That's right. Stars get big old, pop out, top-of-the-line trailers. You know, the kind that they have in "glamorous" trailer parks.

Here's a favorite joke of mine:

> "Question: What's the difference between a Bubba and a Buddy?"
>
> "Answer: A Buddy is a Bubba with a condo."

(If you're an expatriated southerner, that's pretty funny stuff.)

Here's my variation:

> "Question: What do Brad Pitt and a Bubba have in common?"
>
> "Answer: Glamorous accommodations."

☙

Nobody goes to Drama School with the idea of starring in TV commercials when they get out. But guess what?

As the notorious Willie Sutton once said when asked why he robbed banks:

"That's where they keep the money."

Look at it this way. The SAG-AFTRA Commercials Contract runs for a 3-year cycle. It's a billion-dollar contract. That is to say, it generates roughly $333 million in actor income annually.

The TV/Theatrical contract (all Union films and TV shows) generates $650 million in actor salaries over three years. That's approximately $217 million annually.[1]

So, if the Commercials Contract generates $333 million and the TV/Theatrical Contract generates $217 million, that means that collectively Working Actors take home about $550 million in earnings per year (residual payments included).

Using this formula, we can figure out a percentage of the total money earned by Working Actors per year under the SAG-AFTRA Commercials Contract:

$$\frac{\$333 \text{ million (earned per year for commercials)}}{\$550 \text{ million (total earned per year by actors)}} = 60.5\%$$

More than 60% (three-fifths) of all earnings by Working Actors in a given year are derived from TV commercials and residual payments for the reuse of TV commercials.

Clearly, there's a lot of bread to be made in commercials. Shitloads, in fact.

But that being said, I think we can all agree that commercials ain't Art.

In fact, commercials are the antithesis of Art. They're pure commerce. They're complete "pieces of shit." Ergo, 60% of the work performed by Working Actors has nothing whatsoever to do with Art.

Does that mean you should turn your nose up at doing commercials? Fuck, no.

I once saw an interview with the great Christopher Walken. When asked how he chose the "fascinating" parts he plays, Walken replied (and I'm paraphrasing):

"It's not like I had a choice. I played what was offered to me."

Choices are a luxury for the Working Actor. Most of us don't get to make them very often. We scrounge around, looking for work and, like Christopher Walken, we take what we can get. For most of us, that means acting in commercials.

But hey, shooting a commercial sure beats the hell out of waiting tables. It pays better and it's a lot more fun. Plus, it's a great chance to gain some on-camera experience. Every job is a learning opportunity!

If the spot runs at all, the residuals can also buy reams of headshots, pay for classes and fund your "create-your-own" acting projects. Commercial work can also underwrite more pedestrian items like, you know, rent and food.

Commercials also provide the easiest path for actors trying to get started in The Acting Game.

Here's how:

First of all, commercial calls are unlike theatrical auditions in several ways.

Film and TV auditions are usually held in offices or conference rooms. Commercial auditions usually take place concurrently in a rented warren of studios with a large communal waiting area.

It wouldn't be unusual, for instance, for a group of would-be "Silver Foxes" up for a Boner Medication spot to be sharing a waiting room with a few dozen 20-year-old bikini-clad, mini-pad wannabes.

The room can be noisy and (as in this particular case) quite distracting, too. Actors stream in and out of the studios every few minutes. Organized chaos.

This process goes on for hours, usually for multiple days. Commercial Casting Directors can see hundreds of people in a day, no sweat.

Film and TV auditions take quite a bit longer and the producers don't have the time to see as many people. They're busy making their shows. So, the Casting Director has to "cull the herd" before letting them inside the barn.

Due to the smaller number of appointments they can log, theatrical agents sign fewer clients. They try to keep a solid stable of reliable Working Actors who can consistently win jobs.

Commercial agents don't need to be as choosy as theatrical agents. They sign tons of people and submit the hell out of them. The more appointments they get, the better their chances are of grabbing their 10% of the action.

Basically, commercial agents operate on pure greed. They throw clients at the wall and see who sticks. Consequently, commercials provide the easiest path for actors trying to get started in The Game.

If you're just starting out and are looking for representation, getting a commercial agent should be your first priority.

༄

Commercials also help KEEP the Working Actor in the game.

Commercials have sustained many a Working Actor ever since radio was invented. Virtually every Working Actor I know started in commercials.

My first professional job on film was a Panasonic ad for boomboxes. I played a punk rocker. For some reason, they painted my left ear orange. (Ad men are total dorks.)

But hell, it earned me my SAG card.

[Full disclosure: I suck at getting commercials. I once had a Coke audition for an ad that ran and ran and ran. (Dammit.) I was the *only* actor who got called back, but I somehow managed not to get it.]

But listen, lots of Working Actors have launched very successful careers doing commercials.

For instance, I've got this Working Actor buddy. Nicest guy in The Game. When we started out together, he had two little kids so he couldn't afford to be choosy about the parts he'd accept.

The guy would take just about anything that paid Union dollars, but he really struggled. He got the occasional, small, co-star TV part and some regional commercials, but he was always pressed to make ends meet. Then, he won a part in some stinko low-budget war movie that shot in the Philippines.

While he was on location, they gave him a regulation Army flat top. The look worked for him. As soon as he got back to the States, he started booking every commercial he went up for. He cashed in for years.

Then, he parlayed his recognizable face into a contract with a solid theatrical agency. (As we discussed in the previous chapter, he'd made the bastards feel greedy.) It paid off for everyone concerned.

My friend is now playing a leading role on his second consecutive television series. He doesn't go on commercial auditions anymore. He doesn't need to. He's been knocking down series money for seven years now. And counting.

Acting in commercials allowed my pal to stay in The Game. Then, like the ballplayer who kept piling up hits until he reached Cooperstown, my friend kept working.

And he kept right on working until he became a TV Star.

༄

The remaining two-fifths of paid acting work (not counting the Theatre, of course) is on film or TV.

Of the approximately $217 million in actor salaries generated annually from the TV/Theatrical contract, about 60% of that money comes from TV.

That means actors earn, collectively, around $130 million performing on Union television programs (including residuals).[2]

That's 23% of the total monies earned by Working Actors. That's considerably less than half of what's earned by actors doing Union commercials.

While commercials and TV generate a combined $463 million in actor income per annum, film work only accounts for a relatively paltry $87 million. That's only 16% of the yearly take by Working Actors.[3]

If you plan to pay your bills next year as a Working Actor, you're more than five times more likely to earn your cash doing something other than film work. You'll probably end up in a commercial or on a scripted TV show.

The numbers don't lie. TV and commercials: that's where the money is.

☙

I've always loved TV.

The first idea I ever got about becoming an actor came from watching Billy Mumy ("Danger, Will Robinson") on *Lost in Space*.

Kurt Russell was my hero.

For me, getting to work with both William Shatner (on *Boston Legal*) and George Takei (*The Pool Boys*) was like being beamed-up to Heaven.

I love acting on TV. These days, it's the best medium for actors.

Unlike film, TV producers don't have enough money or time to shoot at a bunch of different locations. There are only eight tightly budgeted days, so large stunts and over-the-top special effects are kept to a minimum. There are only so many set-ups and camera moves that can be accomplished in a single day.

That's good news for actors.

It means there are long scenes. Humans actually have to speak to one another to fill the time. There's conflict and resolution. There's almost always something decent to play.

It can be a hell of a lot of fun, too.

Some of the best writers in the country end up writing for Primetime, because that's where the jobs are.

I see great stuff on TV all the time. I've been very fortunate to have won parts that have allowed me to play some beautifully written scenes. My very best work has been on TV.

Television provides the Working Actor with a chance to play The Game at a very high level, an arena in which athletic excellence can be achieved.

Although the subject matter, storylines, acting, directing and production values of TV shows can be amazing, television is mostly a big old "piece of shit."

The major problem with TV is the medium itself.

First of all, commercial TV exists to sell advertising. It doesn't actually matter how good or bad the show is so long as people watch it. The more eyeballs (younger eyeballs preferably) pointed at the screen, the more the networks can charge to air Boner Med commercials, which leads to higher profits.

Of course, executives are happier when an arty show gets an audience (because it makes them feel cool). However, at the end of the day, it's all about the Benjamins. Make money, and you get to keep your salary and your Jag. Lose money, and you might be parking someone else's.

Secondly, the structure of a television show is very confining. An hour program is typically only 42 minutes long. The other 18 minutes are a mix of commercials and network promos for other shows. So, the action unfolds in about two-thirds of an hour.

There's a splashy opening scene to hook the audience, a bunch of exposition, a climactic scene to keep Mom and Pop watching through the ads and ...

CUT TO: Bikini-clad girls selling mini-pads!

There's often some great stuff that happens between the commercial breaks, of course, but the structure of a teleplay is inorganic and phony. It only exists to guide the audience to the Personal Hygiene aisle.

Thirdly, television is ephemeral. Most shows simply don't stand the test of time.

I've appeared on several shows over the years that were so popular that they became "Appointment TV." These programs were considered so good, so *cutting-edge,* that missing them would make you feel very uncool at school or at the office the next morning.

L.A. Law, NYPD Blue, ER, The West Wing and *The X-Files* all fell into this very special category. They generated billions in profits and made international stars of people like George Clooney and Gillian Anderson.

In their primes, these shows were all excellent viewing. They had the best writers, directors, producers, actors and crews that money could buy. But I double dog dare you to flip on TV Land and watch any of those shows. They just don't hold up.

These shows may still be entertaining, and the experience of watching them may be wonderfully nostalgic, but they're of the moment, stuck in their particular place and time. The creators caught lightning in a bottle once upon a time, but that moment has long since passed.

And we're just talking about the handful of truly *excellent* shows.

The only sort of good shows? The mediocre shows? The total "piece of shit" shows? (And I've been in *some, plenty* and *a bunch* of each of those, respectively. The Good, The Bad and the Downright Offensive).

Well, today, most of the enjoyment derived from watching these programs would probably come from poking fun at the haircuts or, possibly, trying to spot actors on the way up in their careers. (I once caught a very young Christopher Walken on the original *Hawaii Five-o*. Pretty cool.)

But, is television Art? Hardly.

While the ultra-rare comedy (*The Andy Griffith Show*, for example) may endure for some time, the dramas (*Matlock* comes to mind) don't.

The Andy Griffith Show may be called a "classic" by many people, but, come on, it's not exactly the Mona Lisa. Will people line up to watch it five hundred years after it was created as they do with da Vinci's painting? Color me dubious.

And *Matlock*? It's an utter "piece of shit."

TV is really a writer-producer's playground. Directors are brought in, sometimes at the last minute, to fulfill the creator's vision.

TV directors are mostly hired guns. They knock down about 40 grand (plus residuals) for an hour network Primetime show and about half that for cable (which generates crap residuals).

Films are a different story.

Film is a director-driven medium, for one thing. In a film, writers have usually been replaced (or banished) by the time shooting starts. The producer facilitates the shooting, but it's the director's show.

Is film Art? Maybe.

There were only a hundred fully budgeted films made in the US in 2014. If we eliminate the "piece of shit" kiddie flicks, comic book popcorners, car chasers, sex romp comedies, horror/slasher pics and any movie that starred either [NAME REDACTED BY MY ATTORNEY] or [NAME REDACTED BY MY OTHER ATTORNEY] or, God forbid, both, we're left with a handful of serious pictures, perhaps.

How many of these films will stand the test of time? One? Two? None?

That's not to say that these movies aren't worth watching or, more to the point, working on. They most certainly are.

I love going to the movies with my kids, loading up on Junior Mints and 8 dollar lemonades and kicking back to watch crap like *Cloudy with Yet Another Chance of Meatballs 6* or *Yogi Bear: Does a Wild Bear Shit in the Woods? Number Two*.

I also had a blast working on *Halloween* with Rob Zombie (who despite his name and appearance, is a real sweetheart, not to mention a major talent). It was one of the most fun and strangely satisfying job experiences I've ever had.

But, come on. These are not great movies by any stretch of the imagination. They're total "pieces of shit."

When I *do* land a film part, the chances are extremely high that my work won't be in one of those movies that will be called a work of Art. And even if I do, there's no guarantee that my part will be challenging enough to stretch my athletic muscles.

So, commercials and TV aren't Art, and, except for the very (and I mean *very*) occasional Theatre production where all the pieces fall together (great writing, a talented director, a visionary producer with money to burn and an inspired cast) or the even rarer film project when all the stars align perfectly, most of the acting we'll do in our lifetimes will have nothing whatsoever to do with Art.

So, for all intents and purposes—

Acting is not an Art form.

༝

If my twenty-something-year-old self were reading this chapter, he'd be really pissed off by now.

"This old fucker is a total asshole! Acting isn't an art form? He's completely out of his fucking gourd. I hate this mofo."

Cool your thrusters, young Skywalker. Jedi Mind Trick, it is.

Every acting challenge is an athletic event. We athletes must overcome certain obstacles in order to perform at the highest level. We need to take the pressure off ourselves. Taking "Art" out of the equation gives the Working Actor power.

Treating every project as if it were just another "piece of shit" releases us from any preconceived notions we may have about the work we're undertaking. It allows us to mentally lower the stakes so that we don't become overwhelmed.

You see, our ego selves may fear that we're not equal to the task of mastering a major work of Art. But hell, we're certainly good enough to hang out in a fucking trailer making some "piece of shit," aren't we?

And we're definitely good enough to walk into those audition rooms, stand on our own two feet and give winning auditions (even when the stakes actually *are* high and we really, really, really, really, really want that fucking part a *whole, whole* lot).

Waiting for Godot may be one of the greatest plays ever written. Some might even argue it's a great work of Art.

Robin Williams didn't approach it that way. He treated like it was another "piece of shit." He said, "Art dies tonight!"

"Killing" Art relieved Williams of the awesome responsibility of trying to fulfill the lofty and unattainable expectations that come with performing a classic like *Godot*. It gave him the power to walk out onto that big stage every night and to give *life* to Samuel Beckett's story to the best of his athletic ability.

Similarly, while we Working Actors may feel intimidated by the thought of acting with a famous star, if we mentally cast that star as just another Working Actor, some "Bubba" who just happens to hang out in a slightly nicer trailer than we do, some "Buddy" who started out as a nobody just like we did, then The Game becomes much more winnable.

So, fuck Art!

The rest of this book will explore how we Working Actors can, as Robin Williams put it so eloquently, "bring life" to our work.

CHAPTER FOUR

The Method(s)

"All this talk about the Method, the Method! WHAT method? I thought each of us had our OWN method!"
—Sir Laurence Olivier

The first thing you need to know about the "Method" is that there is no Method.

I once caught a TV interview with the actor Will Geer. His words made quite an impression on me.

Most people remember Geer as the white-haired, curmudgeonly Grandpa on the '70s TV show, *The Waltons,* but he had an amazing career before that.

Geer went to college on a horticultural scholarship but quickly fell in with the Theatre kids. Upon graduating, he moved to New York and joined the influential Group Theatre. He worked on Broadway, did some radio drama and built a solid film career. Then, due to his politics, Geer got blacklisted. He didn't work for years.

Broke and depressed, Geer moved with his family to Topanga Canyon, California, did some landscaping and formed his own theater, the Theatricum Botanicum. Geer's company, which included several of his blacklisted buddies, performed classic and modern works in a natural outdoor amphitheater. The theater still thrives to this day.

Geer did not appear on screen for more than a decade. Ironically, late in his life, he would be hailed as a "great American" by the same U.S. Congress that had tried to run him out of The Game.

Geer said (again, I'm paraphrasing):

"When kids hear that I studied with Stanislavski, they get all excited and want to talk about the Method. The Method, this. The Method, that. And I tell them that there is no Method. There are lots of different Methods."

೧೨

In *The First Six Lessons*, Richard Boleslavski refers to his acting student as "the Creature." He doesn't even deign to call her an actress, much less an Artist. She's a pile of mush, a lump of clay to be molded and stretched and sculpted under his tutelage.

If you haven't read *Six Lessons*, WTF are you doing reading this crap? Put this aside and come back after you've at least read the basic books by Boleslavski *(The First Six Lessons)*, Slanislavski *(An Actor Prepares)*, Meisner *(Sanford Meisner On Acting)* and Hagen *(Respect for Acting)*.

Welcome back. Now we can talk.

So, what was Boleslavski up to calling this kid, "The Creature?"

He's making the point (with a sledgehammer) that she's not an actress—at least not yet. And, by extension, she's certainly not an Artist. Why? In his view, she doesn't know enough to be called an actress. She doesn't have sufficient knowledge of The Game.

Acting isn't like other professions. Pretty much any chucklehead off the street can call himself an actor. (And they do.)

Imagine what the world would be like if some bozo simply could hang out a shingle that reads: "Doctor," "Dentist" or "Attorney-at-Law" after taking a dozen lessons.

I'm getting a toothache and a touch of cancer just thinking about it. Maybe I should sue somebody.

Hanging out a shingle and calling ourselves *actors* isn't going to cut it either.

There are, of course, a few exceptions—refugees of high school *Grease* productions who get ahead without having a clue.

Usually, they're very young, extraordinarily beautiful and spontaneous individuals who, defying the lottery-sized odds against them, somehow, some way, find their way onto the Big Screen on a wing and a prayer.

There are just enough of these stories to inspire the multitudes of provincial hotties to load up their Econoboxes and leave Bug Tussle for Hollywoodland, "where the streets are paved with gold."

Ironically, it's often the same story for the sons and daughters of Hollywood royalty. How many of those Westside Princes and Princesses (and there are many who try) actually make it?

Hell, a lot of them start out at the top with agents at CAA but then inexorably work their way out of the business. Talent is not something a person can just inherit and neither is a Work Ethic.

The "Creature" who doesn't learn the Fundamentals shows no respect for the profession she's hoping to enter. More importantly, she limits her ability to achieve.

☙

Fellow "Creatures" ...

Let's start at the beginning.

Here's a very incomplete and woefully abridged history of modern American acting, 1923–present:

Constantin Stanislavski brought a troupe from his Moscow Art Theatre to the United States in January of 1923.

Over the next sixteen months, the company performed thirteen plays (in Russian, no less) in a dozen American cities. (Hard to imagine in this day and age.) Actors' Equity Association arranged for Stanislavski to give a series of lectures for Union members.

Will Geer would have been about 21 or 22 at that time and was a Working Actor. It's fair to assume that he came into contact with Stanislavski at that time.

Geer was also a member of the Group Theatre when the approach to acting that came to be known as "The Method" was being developed. So, it's safe to say he knew a thing or two about the subject.

It was during that Moscow Art Theatre trip to America that Stanislavski was commissioned by Little, Brown & Co. to write his autobiography. *My Life in Art* was published in 1926. The book was an immediate bestseller—and it still sells like funnel cakes even today.

Stanislavski was the first acting teacher to create a systemized approach for bringing *life* to the stage. It's impossible to overstate the profound effect that his work had on American acting.

☙

There is no Method. There are lots of different Methods.

Richard Boleslavski, Stanislavski's student, didn't think too highly of the Bolshevik Revolution of 1917. Originally a Pole, he skipped out of Russia after the Revolution and bounced around in Europe before finally landing in New York City. In 1923, he opened the American Laboratory Theatre.

During Stanislavski's Moscow Art Theatre tour of 1923–24, actress and teacher Maria Ouspenskaya defected to the U.S. and joined Boleslavski's Lab.

Known to her students as "Madame," the Lilliputian Ouspenskaya (who would later move her classes to LA, get nominated for two Academy Awards and literally go up in smoke after she went to bed with a bottle of booze and a cigar) was principally responsible for the dissemination of the Stanislavski System to American actors.

Boleslavski (who also died in Hollywood at an early age) may have written his famous *Lessons,* but among Ouspenskaya's 1500-plus students were some of the most influential actors and acting teachers of the early part of 20th century.

Lee Strasberg was one of them.

After a couple of years of study at the Lab under Ouspenskaya, Strasberg partnered up with director Harold Clurman and producer Cheryl Crawford to form The Group Theatre.

Theirs was a novel approach to Theatre in the United States. Their mission was to unite actors, writers and directors and create a socially relevant Theatre.

With Strasberg as its Artistic Director, The Group Theatre would carry the American torch for the Stanislavski System. Teaching what The Group coined "The Method," Strasberg expanded on what he learned in Ouspenskaya's studio and led the company through extensive Affective Memory exercises.

Affective Memory, an important tool in any Working Actor's Skill Set, requires actors to use their own memories to stimulate truthful emotional responses while working on a scene.

The Group's productions were a bit of a hit-and-miss proposition (especially financially). Strasberg, a caustic prophet for his Method, considered audiences to be an annoyance. But under his leadership, The Group was to become the cradle of modern American acting.

Among The Group were three actors who would later become some of the most influential acting teachers of the century: Stella Adler, Sanford Meisner and Robert Lewis.

ಙ

There is no Method. There are lots of different Methods.

The always-glamorous actress Stella Adler and her lover (and eventual husband) Harold Clurman, traveled to Paris in 1934. Through a stroke of good fortune, Stanislavski also happened to be in town, and Adler got a chance to study with the Master for five weeks.

Adler discovered that Stanislavski had changed the focus of his approach.

Whereas before, Stanislavski had stressed Affective Memory in his teaching, he'd come around to the opinion that "Given Circumstances" and "Action and Imagination" were the key components to his system. This, of course, was in direct conflict with what Strasberg was teaching.

When Adler reported her findings to The Group, there was an immediate anti-Method backlash.

Strasberg argued that he wasn't teaching the "Stanislavski Method," he was teaching the "Strasberg Method." However, some of The Group demanded that Adler teach them what she'd learned from the Master.

Stella Adler was launched as an acting instructor.

Instead of working on lessons in Memory, she focused on Script Analysis and Historical Context—the Given Circumstances—and how they related to Action.

Adler once said, "Drawing on the emotions I experienced, for example, when my mother died, to create a role, is sick and schizophrenic. If that is acting, I don't want to do it."

Stanislavski himself had asserted that he had developed Affective Memory as a last resort—for use when an actor couldn't self-stimulate truthful emotions using his own imagination.

Strasberg resigned from The Group Theatre in 1935. Inarguably, though, he was primarily responsible for sowing the seeds of the Stanislavski System in America.

The company's financial troubles (and the lure of Hollywood money for its members) finally led to The Group's breakup just prior to World War II.

After a few detours at other schools, Adler finally opened the Stella Adler Conservatory of Acting in 1949. During her time, she taught over two thousand students, including Brando and DeNiro—guys whose work likely influenced every actor that came after them.

༄

Group Theatre members Sanford Meisner and Robert Lewis were deeply affected by Adler's 1934 revelations.

As he outlined in his 1958 book, *Method–or Madness?*, Lewis felt that Strasberg's Method relied too heavily on the internal, psychological aspects of Stanislavski's System. Lewis favored a more holistic approach.

In 1947, Lewis, Cheryl Crawford and director Elia Kazan started The Actors Studio.

All three were riding high at the time. Kazan had just staged the triumphant *A Streetcar Named Desire* with the young Brando. Crawford and Lewis were just off their very successful Broadway production of *Brigadoon.*

But in 1948, Lewis had a falling out with Kazan and abruptly resigned from The Studio.

Lee Strasberg stepped in, and by 1951, he was in charge. He ran The Actors Studio until his death in 1982.

It bears repeating that this overview of American acting history is just a meager outline. The entire careers and accomplishments of giants have been compressed down to a paltry few sentences.

Here's but a very small sample of the Working Actors who came out of The Actors Studio (a Who's Who of Hollywood Heavyweights):

Robert DeNiro, Al Pacino, Sean Penn, Jack Nicholson, Steve McQueen, Paul Newman, Ellen Burstyn, Anne Bancroft, Faye Dunaway, Marilyn Monroe, Shelley Winters, Anthony Hopkins, Gene Hackman, Harvey Keitel, Dustin Hoffman, Phillip Seymour Hoffman, Sally Field, Christopher Walken, Kevin Spacey, Dennis Hopper, Olympia Dukakis, Sissy Spacek, Geraldine Page, Mickey Rourke, Sidney Poitier, Lee Remick, Julie Harris, Cloris Leachman, Bruce Dern, Karl Malden, Rue McClanahan, Carroll O'Connor and many others.

Enough said. These people stretched the limits of the Acting Game, and they inspired legions of other actors. They changed the course of American acting forever.

ତ

There is no Method. There are lots of different Methods.

Sanford Meisner was one of the first acting instructors at The Actors Studio, but he's mostly remembered for his forty years of work at the Neighborhood Playhouse. Meisner developed a series of repetition exercises that forced the actor to take his attention off of himself and put it onto his acting partners so that *behavior* would drive the Action.

Meisner taught his actors to live truthfully under Imaginary Circumstances, as opposed to The Studio's Method of Affective Memory. He once told Strasberg that the Method "introverted" actors.

Among his many successful students, Meisner taught Gregory Peck, Joanne Woodward, Peter Falk, Jon Voight, Robert Duvall, Diane Keaton and Mary Steenburgen, to name but a few.

It should be noted that many of Meisner's best students, Duvall for instance, were later asked by Strasberg to join The Actors Studio. Meisner felt Strasberg tried to take credit for teaching these star pupils how to act, and it rankled the hell out of him.

⁂

There is no Method. There are lots of different Methods.

When Robert Lewis left The Actors Studio to concentrate on his Broadway directing career, he continued to teach at the Lincoln Center Training Program, the Robert Lewis Theatre Workshop and at several universities, before settling in as Chairman of the Acting and Directing programs at Yale.

On April 15, 1957 at the Playhouse Theatre in New York, Lewis launched a series of eight talks that later became the basis for his book, *Method–or Madness?* Despite the 10:30pm start times of the lectures, over 5,000 Theatre professionals submitted written applications for attendance.

Lewis asserted that it was wrong for teachers of the Method to focus almost exclusively on Stanislavski's Affective Memory techniques while ignoring the Russian master's teachings on the Fundamentals.

Lewis said that Strasberg "ghettoized" American actors, making them incapable of playing characters from different places or in different time periods. Lewis advocated for actor training that included the external Fundamentals of movement, voice and speech as well.

If you've ever caught the work of his star pupil, Meryl Streep, it's pretty clear that Lewis was on to something.

So, even the bona fide geniuses who created and developed the Method vehemently disagreed about what the Method was and how it should be used.

Or, as Will Geer said, "There is no Method."

But let's be clear about one thing:

While there may not be a so-called "Method," you, the Working Actor, definitely need to have some kind of method.

In order to increase your odds of winning at the Acting Game, it is essential that you develop a reliable, repeatable and systematic approach to bringing *life* to your work.

Like Mr. Geer, I'm a Cafeteria Catholic when it comes to the so-called Method. I pick and choose from all the Methods—and then some. I certainly subscribe to Lewis' commitment to training in the Fundamentals and Meisner's approach to Imaginary Circumstances.

From Lloyd Richards, Dean of the Yale Drama School, I picked up an exercise that explores behavior that I find very helpful—especially when it comes to auditioning.

From the Associate Dean, Earle Gister, I learned a valuable process à la Adler that I always use when exploring Given Circumstances.

In the rare instances when I employ Affective Memory, I use a technique taught to me by one of my coaches, Kate McGregor-Stewart.

I stand on the shoulders of giants. In other words, I steal from everybody.

I'll outline these "Methods" in the following chapters, as well as some of my own techniques I've developed in my studio. Here's a little advice before we proceed:

Steal what works for you and shitcan what doesn't.

As Stanislavski himself said:

"Create your own Method. Don't depend slavishly on mine. Make up something that will work for you! But keep breaking traditions, I beg you."

Create your own Method—and don't neglect your Fundamentals.

CHAPTER FIVE

Affective Memory

*"The actor becomes an emotional athlete.
The process is painful—my personal life suffers."*
—Al Pacino

You're an athlete. In order to improve your athletic performance, you need to get out of your head and start developing your acting muscles. A runner will never get out of the starting blocks by merely thinking about the race.

Working Actors aren't like musicians. We *are* our instruments. We "play" our voices and our bodies. We "play" our imaginations.

We can also "play" our experiences.

Our experiences are what shape us. They make us who we are. Our experiences humanize us. They are our keys, our chords and our melody.

What's the most efficient way of putting them to work?

☙

Paul Anderson's film, *Boogie Nights* boasts a superb cast, and is loaded with terrific performances. Don Cheadle, William H. Macy and John C. Reilly are all Working Actors (who later achieved stardom) and each delivers solid support to Mark Wahlberg. Julianne Moore, who is always fucking brilliant, is simply off the charts in this one. Burt Reynolds gives the best performance of his life.

Nominally, the film is a look at the porn industry in the Disco Age. Thematically, however, it's a crazy riff on the family unit.

Wahlberg plays Dirk Diggler, a teen slacker at odds with his mom. Blessed with huge "talent," he catches the eye of Reynolds, the Porn King. Reynolds and Moore assume the role of parents to young Dirk and, indeed, to all their porn star and crew member "children."

In Dirk's remarkable first scene before the porn lens, he earnestly seeks Moore's approval as he lays her out across a desk, and she, a woman who has lost her family because of her career choice and her drug addiction, reassures him in a gentle, maternal way. All the while, he's fucking her onscreen for money. It's mind-bending stuff from a pair of very brave actors.

Philip Seymour Hoffman not only had trouble getting arrested as an actor when he first started out, but also couldn't manage to hold down the shit jobs he had to take as a waiter or a lifeguard.

After landing a nice supporting part in *Scent of a Woman*, opposite Al Pacino, he never had to look for another survival job. However, it wasn't until he wound up playing Scotty J., the closeted Production Assistant/Boom Operator in *Boogie Nights,* that he truly entered the consciousness of the American moviegoing public.

☙

There's an old joke:

> "Question: How many actors does it take to screw in a light bulb?"
>
> "Answer: A thousand. One to do the job and 999 to say, 'I could have done it better.'"

It's only funny because it's true.

I doubt there's an actor in the world who hasn't watched some other joker in a movie and thought, "Hell, I should be playing that part." (Our good pal Crazy Ass Bruce never saw a project in his life without thinking that.) I've done it too, more times than I care to count.

But watching Philip Seymour Hoffman in *Boogie Nights,* I had a very different reaction.

Hoffman's performance in the early part of the film is fine. He does some shameless stuff with a ballpoint pen to telegraph his sexual issues. Later, we watch as he struggles to fit in with the cool-guy porn stars in spite of his awkward, overweight physique. Pretty good stuff.

But it's not until later in the film, when he lures Dirk out to the driveway during the fateful New Year's party on the pretext of showing off his new car and subsequently tries to kiss him, that Hoffman reveals his Emotional Skill Set.

Rejected by a revolted Dirk, Scotty melts down with an acute embarrassment that transmogrifies into a deep, self-loathing agony. His need for Dirk's love is so focused, that even as he's backpedaling and apologizing, he somehow manages to continue to stay the aggressive pursuer. He's sweating and his skin begins to mottle. His stench is palpable.

In the end, Scotty is only able to get a friendly hug from Dirk, who can't get back to the party fast enough. Scotty winds up alone in his shiny new, red sports car, wallowing in total humiliation and wailing over and over, "I'm a fucking idiot. I'm a fucking idiot. I'm a fucking idiot ..."

Until that climactic moment, Scotty J. is a comic character. He's a buffoonish, trying-too-hard fat kid in a tank top that's two sizes too small for him. Suddenly, out of nowhere, we see him for what he is: a lonely, desperate and painfully needy man. His humanity is revealed in an instant.

There isn't a person alive who hasn't suffered that kind of rejection. It's mortifying. In adolescence, each of us makes clumsy attempts at getting the love we crave, and we've all been shot down in flames. It's part of growing up, and it hurts like hell.

As an audience, we are lulled by Hoffman's disarming, goofy performance. In the next breath, however, we get slapped upside the head with his reality. We identify with him, because each of us has felt his excruciating shame before. For that moment, we are *all* Scotty J., the gay chubby porn nerd, because each of us can recognize his all-too-human anguish within ourselves.

This is why we go to the movies.

అ

Joseph Campbell, the renowned scholar of comparative mythology and religion, once said:

"People say that what we're all seeking is a meaning for life. I don't think that's what we're really seeking. I think that what we're seeking is an experience of being alive, so that our life experiences on the purely physical plane will have the resonances within our own innermost being and reality, so that we actually feel the rapture of being alive."[4]

The Rapture of being alive!

This is the reason we huddle in the dark movie temples and inhale our pails of popcorn and half-gallon Diet Cokes like they're Holy Communion. We need actors like Philip Seymour Hoffman to remind us what it feels like to be *alive*.

That Hoffman is still able to achieve this feat, even in death, is a living testament to his monumental talents as a Working Actor.

☙

Instead of mentally firing Philip Seymour Hoffman and projecting myself into his part (as per usual) I was simply blown away. I could actually sense the guy's blood pressure rising during that scene.

A split second later, I remember thinking, "How the hell did he do that? I can't do that. Compared to him, *I'm* the fucking idiot."

Mind you, I was working like a crazy man at that time. I was a very busy Working Actor. In that instant, however, it became crystal clear to me that if I intended to continue working, I was going to have to get better. A lot better. I needed to improve my Emotional Skill Set.

So once again, I put my sorry ass back into acting class.

☙

I met Kate McGregor-Stewart through Marisa Tomei. Kate has been coaching Marisa for decades, and Marisa often takes her along on location for films like *The Wrestler*. A Working Actor herself, Kate was in the same Yale class as Meryl Streep and Sigourney Weaver during Robert Lewis' time.

A single mom and congenital Earth Mother, Kate cuts a very maternal swath in the acting studio. She's all red ringlets, drapey clothes and clogs. She's into herbs and crystals and chanting and self-help seminars and all kinds of other stuff that clashes with my own more secular sensibilities. Yet there's something infectious about Kate's unfailingly positive approach to life (and to show business in particular) that deeply resonates with me. She is simply impossible to resist. Kate's the good witch.

She's also one of the most innovative acting coaches to come along for quite some time.

Kate teaches a quick-and-easy, down-and-dirty approach to Affective Memory. She calls the exercise, "Sentence Completions." She spends some time on it at the beginning of every class. She'll read out a sentence like:

"I feel guilty that _____ ."

If you're in a state of Relaxed Concentration, your body will have an immediate emotional response to a word like "guilty."

Do the exercise for yourself:

Say, "I feel guilty that _____" to yourself and take a minute to recognize the various sensations in your body and on your skin. It's likely that you'll feel the sensations of guilt before you're even able to pinpoint the exact memory from which your guilt presently emanates.

Describe the sensations you're feeling aloud. Finish the exercise by saying, "I feel guilty that _____." And fill in the blank.

Here's my own response:

Intense heat spreads across my chest and abdomen. It's as if I'm sitting too close to a space heater. Saliva burns in my mouth. My head grows heavy and collapses towards my chest. My eyes are jumping around. They won't stay still. There's a large hand pushing down on my breastbone. I feel guilty that I DIDN'T FIGHT HARDER FOR CRYSTAL.

Notice that I speak in the present tense. When doing this exercise, don't describe how you felt at some point in the past. Use whatever comes up for you and experience it in the here-and-now.

Here are some more powerful Sentence Completions you should try:

I feel love at first sight when _____.

I'm terrified that _____.

I am full of hope that _____.

I am destroyed by _____.

I am filled with rage when _____.

I am completely humbled by _____.

There are an almost unlimited number of sentences that you can use to help you sharpen your Emotional Skill Set. It's a very practical exercise, and you can work on it alone. You don't need a partner. You don't need a class. If you come up against a difficult moment while shooting a scene, you can take a couple of minutes to self-stimulate a truthful, emotional response using your own memories.

Take 10 minutes every day to do a Sentence Completion. Give your acting muscles a workout. Develop your Emotional Skill Set.

☙

Unlike Stella Adler, who felt that drawing on emotions she experienced during traumatic events in her life was "sick and schizophrenic," I'll use whatever I need to use to get the job done. While I mainly rely on my Imagination to create a fertile set of Given Circumstances and specific Imaginary Circumstances that will allow me to live truthfully (subjects for later chapters) my experiences, both joyful and tragic, make me who I am. They're unique to me. They're mine. And I'll use them as I damn well please.

What follows is a story from my personal experience that demonstrates how I use Affective Memory in my own work.

Please keep in mind, I'm not writing this down because I want your sympathy or because I want you to think I'm a good guy. I'm telling you this story because that's what Working Actors do. We reveal ourselves. We expose ourselves. We confess. We invite people into the shadowy recesses of our beings and we let them poke around.

Actors are vampires, only we suck the blood out of our *own* lives—from our experiences and our imaginations. Then, we smear our emotional and psychological gore all over the screen to help remind people what it feels like to be *alive*.

If we get to be good enough at it, it'll also pay the bills.

☙

CRYSTAL AND ME

(An Autobiography)

I remember a joke my high school buddy (known at that time as Captain Crude) made up after Sex Ed (which, comically, was taught by a bent old priest):

"There's a vas deferens between boys and girls."

For those of you who skipped school that day, the "vas deferens" is the tubing that carries sperm from the scrotum on its way to exciting ports of call in the wide world beyond. Women don't have one. Hence, the joke.

I, like a slim minority of other men, don't have one either. It's something of a joke, to be sure, but not a particularly funny one if procreation happens to be your bag (so to speak). It's the equivalent of being born with a congenital vasectomy.

I was unaware that I had this condition, but it likely saved me from several disastrous parallel lives that I might have lived due to my collegiate libertinism.

The town where I grew up was a couple of decades back-to-the-future. The Sexual Revolution was as remote as the French one. The populace was deeply Puritanical, full of folks who, as H.L. Mencken once famously said, lived with "the haunting fear that someone, somewhere, may be happy."

Add to that mix a cup-and-a-half of Catholic School education, and you can imagine that pussy was pretty hard to come by. Once emancipated from those strict confines, it seemed a duty to disseminate my seed as widely (yet thinly) as was humanly possible.

I had never harbored even the remotest interest in becoming a parent, in any case, and only discovered my lack of ductwork after my first wife's gynecologist insisted that I be tested, for fear that my wife might have some disease or other.

Having scoped out a doctor I found in the Yellow Pages (Weinstein, S., chosen for his no-nonsense lack of a first name), I dutifully made love to a sterile baby food jar and quickly made my bemused way (by subway, I shit you not) to the lab, carrying my "pureed cauliflower" in a brown lunch bag.

The results were neither surprising nor particularly earth-shattering—to me at least. However, various family members had apparently harbored pastel dreams of Elmo mobiles, yellow ducky wallpaper borders and full-to-the-brim Diaper Genies. To them, my paternal sitcom was a Jacobean horror story.

A year or so later, when it was suggested to me that we might adopt a child from the woefully inept Los Angeles County foster system, I decided to go along for the ride. Everyone seemed to want it. It also appealed (I'm ashamed to admit) to my East Coast, Ivy League, liberal sensibilities.

I cannot recall if (given my self-absorbed, seat-of-my pants approach to existence) it ever occurred to me that other people's lives might be at stake.

Skipping ahead in the story (leaving out reams of paperwork, fingerprinting, various home inspections, tedious meetings with droning functionaries and parenting classes that prepared one for virtually nothing), we received a call one night from out of the blue. They were bringing us a kid. They'd be there in fifteen minutes. Were we home?

So, in the approximate amount of time required to fill a standard baby food container, I became a father.

Crystal was six. When the car pulled up, she was sound asleep in a booster seat. A black Hefty bag containing all her worldly possessions slouched beside her.

Some people will tell you that the love you feel for an adopted child is neither as deep nor as intense as the love you can have for a child that is of your own body. They believe that it is blood that binds us. My experience tells me that they are unequivocally wrong.

In the thirty seconds or so that I stood watching the child sleep, her head lolled to the side, her face untroubled by dreams or worry, I fell in love.

I feel love at first sight when _____.

Something warm breaks loose inside my chest, and rushes up my neck and across my scalp. I've forgotten how to breathe. I'm transfixed and utterly powerless. I feel love at first sight when I SEE THOSE TINY SNEAKERS SPLAYED OUT ACROSS THE BACKSEAT OF THE CAR.

☙

Crystal was not a delicate thing. She had a solid swimmer's body. Her face was square but symmetrical. Her slightly fleshy cheeks and perfect upturned nose were strewn with a sparse constellation of freckles. Her hair was a flat, brown mess. It looked like she had cut it herself with stubby school scissors.

Six months prior, she'd been living in a battered van on the streets of Long Beach with her drug-addicted parents and three younger siblings. A fight erupted between Mommy and the man in charge of bringing Mommy her "medicine." The cops intervened, and the entire brood (ages 9 months to 6 years) landed in the system.

Crystal got deposited in a rough and tumbledown group home. There she was essentially warehoused—given the basic essentials necessary for survival and little else. Mom and Pop Dope Fiend made a few desultory gestures towards reconciliation before, predictably, completely disappearing.

Crystal was an exuberant and passionate child. She was louder than hell. Her laugh exploded out of her in great blasts. If she, say, skinned her knee, the peal that would emanate from her would alert everyone within a two square mile radius.

Crystal had extraordinary depths of energy and charisma, and it was infectious. After spending thirty seconds in her presence, strangers would trot away with an extra little spring in their stride.

Crystal was also, understandably, a big old bag of crazy.

With her parents either M.I.A. or nodding on dope, Crystal had become the de facto mother of her younger siblings. She had been raising an infant, a toddler and her five-year-old autistic brother.

Food had been scarce, and consequently she was obsessed by it. At our house, she would often eat so much that she'd make herself sick. We'd find rotting fruit and stolen cookies squirreled away in odd corners of her room. She'd ask ten times a day what we were having for dessert that night.

Crystal also played wicked head games. Her affections would come crashing towards us and then just as quickly recede in a riptide. She would say sweetly, "Can I call you *Daddy?*" Invariably though, within hours (and sometimes minutes) she'd follow up such delicious declarations with an equally earnest, "You're not my Dad!"

Crystal was, alternately, entirely too knowledgeable for her age and frighteningly immature. Almost daily, she would throw violent tantrums more suitable to a three-year-old. She'd swing her fists and kick the walls, tears spewing from her eyes, snot coursing down her chin.

Once, minutes before a very rare visit from her downtrodden County Social Worker, Crystal tried to throw herself out of the window.

The harried, dead-eyed government woman arrived to find me holding Crystal tightly in my arms, as the child, cursing like a convict, punched at my head with her tiny mitts.

I'm terrified that _____.

My chin aches from being headbutted. I'm hyperventilating and my chest is soaked with tears. Funky kid sweat rises off her pink t-shirt. My right arm is bleeding from the scratches. I'm terrified that THEY'LL TAKE HER AWAY FROM ME.

☙

My wife and I were not prepared for this. Then again, nobody could have been prepared for Crystal. We worked at it, though. We got a basket, put her name on it and filled it daily with bananas, apples and crackers, and told her she could eat from it at any time, day or night. She eventually stopped hoarding, though she obsessively checked on that basket throughout the day for a good long time.

Nominally a first grader, Crystal had no education to speak of. Her access to books had been limited, and she couldn't read. She even spelled her name wrong. Yet, she was precociously intuitive and eager to learn.

Crystal's teacher, Mrs. O'Brien, was a fifty-something, seen-it-all veteran of the crappy Pasadena school system. She was everything that's right about a public school education (and a good argument in favor of human cloning). Crystal took to Mrs. O'Brien as if the woman were her long-lost Grandma. In no time, Crystal was reading up a storm and even was made "Student of the Month."

We were intensely proud of Crystal and head-over-heels in love, but it was exhausting beyond belief. She'd save up all of her tension at school and then fire it at us point-blank at home as soon as she blasted through the front door.

The marriage suffered. Instead of bringing my wife and I closer as a couple, Crystal was a gale that blasted the topsoil off of our relationship, revealing the fissures and faults hidden beneath the seemingly smooth surface.

But my wife and I persevered, settling into a day-to-day routine that, despite the manic outbursts and marital grudges, began to work. Months slipped by, though the days often felt endless. We took Crystal along on our annual East Coast holiday junket, and she slid neatly into the family.

Some weeks later, I remember watching Crystal with sublime satisfaction as she buzzed around the driveway on her new bike, training wheels screaming, pursued by our pack of grinning dogs, her face a wide-open mask of exquisite joy.

Here was a child who, for perhaps the first time in her life, was getting to experience childhood. For that brief instant, I envisioned a future for Crystal that included proms and college, marriage and babies, even a useful, enjoyable occupation. In short, I could see a happy life ahead for Crystal and, by extension, for us.

I'm full of hope that _____ .

Heat spreads across the back of my scalp and my ears tingle. I am as light and airy as a wispy cloud. I might float away. I'm full of hope that IT'S GOING TO WORK OUT AFTER ALL.

☙

Soon after, though, the dream went up in smoke.

The drab skin-and-bones from the Adoption Bureau that gave us Crystal, regretted to inform us that the County of Los Angeles had, in its infinite wisdom, decided to take her back. With a heavy cross weighing down her scrawny neck, she mistily explained to us that Family Reunification was the stated policy of the system.

No, Mr. and Mrs. Crackhead hadn't reemerged from the Lower Depths. The couple that had taken in Crystal's baby siblings wanted to keep them. They wanted them so badly, in fact, that when the County told them that they had to take in all four of the kids, they reluctantly agreed. It was the worst kind of fucking blackmail.

The couple could either take in an autistic 5-year-old and an unstable 6-year-old, or the County would steal their babies. Family Reunification, don't you know. Never mind that it was a recipe for disaster, the County got to perk up its Family Reunification stats and the dead-eyed County Social Worker scored a gold star in her employment file for a job well done.

A judge had already signed the papers. There was nothing to be done. If we didn't give her up willingly, a Sheriff's Deputy would come to the house and take her.

"It's a bad scene. You don't want to do that to her," quoth the Raven.

Two days later, Crystal was gone. She grinned and waved as the woman drove her away. With her natty new suitcase propped beside her, Crystal looked … hopeful.

As Crystal disappeared around the corner and out of my life, I discarded my mask of brave reassurance and stumbled away. More than anything, I wanted to roll on the ground and beat the earth to rubble. I didn't.

Standing in the shower later, I heard a horrific noise: The anguished cry of an injured animal.

It was coming from me.

I'm destroyed by _____.

My head pitches back, my jaw unhinges towards the ceiling. Lava sears my lungs. I'm about to vomit up hot nails. I'm destroyed by THE IMAGE OF HER HOPEFUL LITTLE FACE SLIDING AWAY FROM ME.

☙

My wife and I went into therapy with a dowdy (yet somehow sexy) fifty-something-year-old woman who was so brilliant that had she won a MacArthur Fellowship (AKA the "Genius Grant.")

"You've changed," my wife once said in session. It was an indictment.

"And you've stayed exactly the same," said the wise (and strangely attractive) Dr. Sensible-Shoes to my wife.

And there it was. The crux. The tipping point. Both of them were right. I had changed. My wife had remained the same.

So, I ended up alone.

☙

I worked on the first season of the Amazon Prime series, *Bosch*, based upon the bestselling novels by the affable genius, Michael Connelly. His creation, L.A. Homicide Detective Harry Bosch, is the son of a murdered prostitute. Bosch struggles against his personal demons and the bureaucracy, to hunt down hardcore killers.

A dog digs up the grave of a child. Forensics indicate that the boy has been dead for 20 years. His bones show signs of severe trauma, suggesting that he was routinely abused prior to his murder. The cold trail leads to the boy's father, played by yours truly.

A former TV Star, I'm a broken down old drunk employed at a skanky golf course. When confronted by Bosch, *guilt* overcomes me. I confess, even though I didn't commit the crime.

My lines read, *"What did I do? What did I do?"* That's a question I often ask myself when thinking about Crystal.

In a later episode, the script required me to writhe on the ground, *destroyed* by grief, in front of my son's tiny coffin.

I've trained myself how to self-stimulate truthful, emotional responses in a matter of seconds. I *know* how grief burns inside my body. And I'm not afraid to expose it.

I carried Crystal's picture in my pocket that day. It got me to where I needed to go.

I confess: I've allowed myself to be destroyed on film for money over and over again. Does that make me sick? Schizophrenic? Yeah, maybe. But that's *my* choice.

I'm looking at Crystal's picture right now. Her image stirs up intense feelings and profound memories. It's a reminder that I have lived.

༄

I once had the great good fortune to attend a weekend seminar with Lee Strasberg, Harold Clurman and several other members of The Actors Studio. I can't recall everyone who was there with them but Strasberg's daughter, Susan, was among the group, as was the actor Kevin McCarthy.

Both Clurman and Strasberg were approaching the ends of their lives. (Clurman would die a year or so later in 1980 and Strasberg in 1982.)

Mr. Strasberg was a kindly old gent—at least he was that weekend. His famous temper was never on display. He gently guided a small group of kids through some rudimentary acting exercises.

One girl was trying her damnedest to capture the Master's attention, stomping around, huffing and generally making a massive butthole out of herself. Instead of giving her a deservedly swift kick in the pants, he quietly coaxed her back to reality. It was a mitzvah.

I can still hear the calm, protective lilt in Strasberg's voice. I am jealous now (as I was then) of those actors who got to study with him.

The following day, Clurman delivered one of his legendary speeches. He was all fire and brimstone—a perfect vision of old Moses on the Mount. With his right hand raised above his head like a talon, he roared, thundered, and then decrescendoed to a barely-audible whisper, forcing me to lean forward.

I feel the Rapture when _____.

I'm sitting in the next-to-last row of a darkened theater. I can feel the fabric of the dark, blue seats hot against my thighs, a sea of heads in my way. The hair on my forearms tingles, as if I'm about to be struck by lightning. Does this glowing madman realize that he's no longer facing the audience? Tears push at the back of my eyes, trying to escape. My head is tilted back and my mouth is agape. My hand shoots up to cover it. I'm afraid I might cry out, "Hallelujah!"

I feel the Rapture when I HEAR HAROLD CLURMAN'S VOICE.

☙

There are times when being a Working Actor comes at a steep price. Writing this chapter, reliving these events, has caused me tremendous personal discomfort. At times, it has been very painful. But these memories are examples of some of the very rare moments in my life in which I felt truly *alive*.

Affective Memory can be a powerful weapon in your Working Actor's Skill Set. Use it.

You're an emotional athlete. Develop your skills. Have courage. Don't be afraid to expose your humanity.

CHAPTER SIX

Imagination

*"I believe in imagination.
I did Kramer vs. Kramer before
I had children. But the mother
I would be was already inside me."*
—Meryl Streep

There are two ways to prepare for a scene. We've studied Affective Memory. Now let's have a look at Imaginary Circumstances.

One day, I was coaching a talented, young Working Actor. She was struggling mightily with self-doubt. She would thoroughly prepare for her auditions (a subject for future chapters). She'd show up ready (ditto). But somewhere between the parking lot and the audition room, she'd lose it. She'd fall prey to her negative thoughts and blow the audition. It kept happening time after time.

"Imagine this," I said to her. "You're Serena Williams. Serena shows no fear."

The response in her body was automatic. She immediately sat up straighter. She had fire in her guts. She looked fierce. She was powerful. She *was* Serena.

My suggestion took her out of her head. Her imagination completely bypassed her consciousness, and she had an instant, truthful, emotional response based solely upon the Imaginary Circumstances I had given her. And her feelings were absolutely real. Her response was as truthful as any reaction she might have self-stimulated using her own experiences through Affective Memory.

Try it. Pick an athlete. You're Serena. You're Tom Brady. You're LeBron. Try them on for size. I'll bet you a buck your body had an immediate emotional response. Were those feelings "real" to you? I'll bet you three more bucks they were.

How does Serena enter Centre Court at Wimbledon? How does Brady walk into Gillette Stadium? How does LeBron come into every NBA arena?

Like they fucking own the place.

Affective Memory isn't the only tool that we Working Actors can use to self-stimulate truthful emotions in our bodies. We can also use our Imaginations.

Personally, I prefer the Imagination approach. While Affective Memory can help a Working Actor build his Emotional Skill Set and exercise his acting muscles, I don't usually find it necessary to use while I'm working. Many of the scenes I play aren't exactly "High Drama." I can easily self-stimulate a truthful preparation using Imaginary Circumstances. And it causes no damage to my psyche.

Depending upon the demands of the scene you're playing, choose the technique the works best for you.

Meisner taught his students to live truthfully under Imaginary Circumstances. He called this approach, "the Magic As-If."

"So preparation is like daydreaming," Meisner said. "It *is* daydreaming. It's daydreaming which causes a transformation in your inner life, so that you are not what you actually were five minutes ago, because your fantasy is working on you."[5]

For example, say you're playing the following scene:

You've just found out you're pregnant and you're coming into a restaurant for lunch with your best friend. You're bursting to tell her the good news.

Well, you've never been pregnant before. You don't know how it feels to find out that you're pregnant. (In fact, the concept may be repellant to you.) Without indicating a fake and unspecific version of joy, how do you create a truthful emotional response in your body?

That's where the "Magic As-If" comes into play. You can create a scenario that will trigger a similar response. For example.

It's "as-if" you just found out you won the part you auditioned for yesterday.

For the Working Actor, *getting the job* is an awesome daydream. It elicits an immediate emotional response. Try it on for size. Say it out loud:

"I just got the fucking job!"

Dollars to [gluten-free] doughnuts, you had a joyful, emotional response. Take note of where you felt it in your body. That's where *your joy* lives. You can call it up anytime you need it.

Instead of bringing a generalized concept of what joy is into the scene, you can now enter the restaurant with a wide range of truthful passions roiling in your body.

Those specific feelings are unique to you and they're very real. You've now prepared yourself to play the scene truthfully.

Try these out. Say the following statements aloud:

It's *as-if* I just found sexual texts on my lover's phone.

It's *as-if* my sister just had a baby.

It's *as-if* I've just learned that Mom has a tumor.

It's *as-if* I found 3000 bucks in a bag on the street.

It's *as-if* my landlord just evicted me from my home.

These are powerful statements that are likely to elicit strong emotional responses. And the best part is—no one will know which technique you used to prepare. No one will care. They'll just see a Working Actor living truthfully. These circumstances are very real to you, but they're your secret. They're your own "method."

☙

There's virtually no limit to the number of useful Imaginary Circumstances you can work with. You're only confined by the boundaries of your own imagination. If a scene isn't working for you, change your Preparation. Create a new set of Imaginary Circumstances for yourself.

For instance, in Studio A, the lab I created while writing *The Working Actor,* a talented ballplayer-turned-actor was struggling with Christopher Durang's *Beyond Therapy,* a humorous (but dated) play about a straight-curious gay man, Bruce (yes, another Bruce!) who meets a slightly neurotic woman, Prudence, through the personal ads.

The actor, a towering and muscular straight guy, approached his acting partner with the sort of manly confidence that he has probably used quite successfully in dozens of bars in the real world. Emotionally, nothing was happening. The scene was painfully unfunny.

Finally, we came up with a set of Imaginary Circumstances that got him headed in the right direction:

"It's *as-if* you're in eighth grade and you're talking to an actual girl for the first time in your life and—not only that—she's actually talking back to you."

Suddenly, this super-male athlete felt quite insecure. He was awkward in his body. He felt desperate to be liked, and he started trying too hard to impress her.

For Prudence, the same "as-if" worked beautifully. The actress, feeling gawky and inadequate as any 13-year-old girl would, was lovably dorky. Her shocked, vulnerable reaction when she learned that Bruce was gay was hilarious.

☙

The "Magic As-If" can be invaluable when preparing for auditions. We Working Actors don't have much time to get ready. It can help cut through a lot of preconceived intellectual "choices." It allows the athlete in us to do the work we have been trained to do.

(By the way, "choices" is a term I've grown to hate. More on this in a later chapter.)

Once upon a time, I was coaching a well-established Working Actor who was reading for a recurring part on a TV series. It was a great part and it would have paid him a lot of money. He was delirious to get it.

The character is a wizened old hippie living in a trailer in the middle of the desert who sells rocks for a living. And mummified animal remains. In short, the guy's a weirdo. He's also something of a mystic. The lead character appears at the hippie's door, and they have a freaky conversation, the hippie offering cryptic advice to the younger man.

The actor came to me very focused on the external eccentricities of the part. He had props with him and was wearing some sort of bullshit costume. His acting was all over the place. It took me quite a while to talk him down off the ledge.

"Look," I said. "They aren't going to care about all that shit. They want to see *you*. And, believe me, you're weird enough! What they want to see is the relationship between you and the kid. This is what this scene is about: It's *as-if* a young actor has come to you to ask your advice on how to play Hamlet."

Suddenly, the lights came on. His behavior, while still rather peculiar, was focused. He had purpose. He was able to play the scene truthfully using the Imaginary Circumstances we had discovered together.

They later offered him the part.

༒

We Working Actors often face difficult challenges in our work.

I once played a role in a very forgettable, "piece of shit" TV series called *Eleventh Hour*. (It was so forgettable, in fact, that I had to pull up my resume on IMDb to remember its freakin' name.)

I am a scientist who accidentally gets poisoned with methamphetamine. I go nuts. Eventually, convinced that "they" are after me, I crash my Jeep into a front-end loader and I'm decapitated. (TV— gotta love it.)

A scene like this provides a unique set of problems.

I've never been high on meth. (I swear, Ma!) I have no idea what it feels like nor do I care to find out.

Sure, I can look up the symptoms of meth overdose on the Web. There's a laundry list of stuff: agitation, chest pains, organ damage, seizure, stroke, heart attack, delusional behavior, extreme paranoia and mood swings. (Gee, sounds like a blast, huh? Let's party down with some meth!)

Obviously, it's impossible to play all that crap. It's overwhelming.

First, I worked on cottonmouth as a symptom. (It's not on the list but I know what it feels like from my pot smoking days.) It affected my speech and my behavior, and it also helped propel the story forward by making me drink more and more of the tainted water that contained the drug.

Second, I developed some Imaginary Circumstances.

When I was young, I had a recurring nightmare that a stranger was in my house and coming to get me. In my dream, I would "wake up" in pitch black and try to turn on the lamp ... but it wouldn't light. I would run to the wall switch ... but the lights wouldn't work. "He's going to get me!" And then I would wake up for real, utterly terrified.

I had this dream so many times that eventually I began to recognize it as a dream. Sometimes I'd wake up screaming, "Wake up! Wake up!"

So, I played my dry-mouthed death scene *as-if* I were stuck in my dream and fighting to wake up.

The "as-if" affected my behavior in many ways, obviously. My paranoia made me extremely agitated. I was hyperventilating. I felt like I might have a heart attack. My desperation to wake up was real enough to force me to jump behind the wheel of a car and smash head-on into another vehicle.

So, my "as-if" scenario created in me a host of feelings similar enough to the symptoms of meth overdose that allowed me to play the scene honestly.

∽

I highly recommend re-reading the chapters on Preparation in *Sanford Meisner on Acting*. Imagination is a critical component in developing your Emotional Skill Set. The "Magic As-If" is a great tool for you to use anytime and anywhere. And as you can see, its results can be quite powerful.

Harnessing the power of your Imagination will help you get out of your head, and it will free the athlete in you to perform to the best of its ability.

CHAPTER SEVEN

The Behavior of Our Scene Partners

> *"If only we could pull out
> our brains and use only our eyes."*
> —Pablo Picasso

Everything we've talked about so far is all about you.

Your Fundamentals. *Your* Emotional Skill Set. *Your* Imagination. *Your* Preparation. But, guess what? You have a scene partner. And she has issues, too.

Meisner once said: "For an actor, Preparation is warming up." That bears repeating:

Preparation is warming up.

Let's say you're playing that restaurant scene with your best friend. (The same scene from Chapter 6). You've just learned that you're pregnant.

You've worked up a Preparation using Imaginary Circumstances (it's *as-if* you've just found out that you've won that role you really wanted). You're all "warmed up."

You skip into the restaurant, dying to convey the good news.

But you enter to find your best friend in tears. Her longtime boyfriend has been sleeping with someone else. (That fucker!)

Only a sociopath would continue with this joyful Preparation under these circumstances.

Your best friend is in deep despair. You can't be over the moon, you have to console your besty. You've got to deal with the *behavior* in front of you.

So, all that Preparation you worked so hard on goes *poof,* right out the window. You've got to let it all go and *act*.

A lot of actors make the mistake of holding on to their Preparation. (Sometimes for dear life.)

I once coached a guy for an audition. We worked up a very emotional Preparation using Affective Memory. The scene really soared in the Studio. He left on a major high, primed to kick some ass and win the job.

But he called me afterward, very distraught. He'd blown the audition.

"I don't know what happened," he said, the words tumbling out of his mouth.

"I was all prepared and everything. I was really worked up. I started great, and then, like, all of a sudden, nothing was happening. So, I started trying to do it like I did when we worked on it. Then,

I just sucked. And at the end, she was all, *'Next!'* What the fuck is wrong with me, Pat?"

Finally, after talking him off the ledge (convincing him that, no, he didn't "suck" and, no, he shouldn't "quit the fucking business") I asked him what the reader was wearing. He had no idea.

In fact, apart from recalling that the reader was a woman, he couldn't describe her at all. He had been so focused on his own Preparation that he had forgotten that there was someone else in the scene.

Of course, nothing was "happening." He was playing the scene with himself!

☙

Elia Kazan, Co-Founder of The Actors Studio, once said:

"[Meisner's students] were the best ... they were both sensitive inside, and they were free as far as their external behavior went. Sometimes you'd get some actors who were taught the so-called Method, which is a term I hate, but they were as if they were playing scenes with themselves." [6]

Playing with oneself isn't Acting.

Let's say you've prepared emotionally to play a scene. Either you've employed Kate McGregor-Stewart's "Sentence Completion" exercise in Affective Memory or you've built up a series of "Imaginary Circumstances" à la Meisner or you've used some crazy ass shit that you learned at the Theatre of the Busted Commode. You've got to *do* something with all this stuff.

You don't want to, as Kazan said, play the scene with yourself. There's a word for this that Kazan is simply too much of a gentleman to use. It's called "masturbation."

I've got nothing against rubbing one off, mind you. It's the best argument I can think of in favor of the evolution of the opposable thumb.

But emotional masturbation is a trap.

While it may be thrilling to self-stimulate our emotions and to give ourselves interior hand jobs, endlessly playing with our feelings and wallowing around in our emotional jism isn't acting.

It's self-indulgent crap.

For instance, I saw a woman give a studio performance as Masha in Chekhov's *The Three Sisters* that absolutely blew me away.

Her sexual desire for Vershinin was so raw, so intense, that had it not been for her remarkably graceful body and demure countenance, it would have been very awkward to watch. The actress brought so much carnal need into the scene that it took everything in her power to control herself.

After the class, I walked out into the crisp, autumn morning convinced I'd seen the next coming of Meryl Streep.

My former classmates and I still talk about her performance to this very day.

But, unfortunately, the actress was never that good again. Her work became increasingly erratic and self-involved. She'd mumble her way through scenes, crying at inappropriate moments. It was as if she were alone on stage.

Later, her introverted emotional life began to manifest itself in a very public way. She developed a peculiar habit of touching her own body in a sexual way every time she got up to work.

She was completely lost in herself.

Why the teacher didn't yell, "Hey, get your hands off your jugs and act!" I'll never know. Maybe he was too embarrassed.

This actress never became Meryl Streep. As far as I know, she's not even in the business anymore. A terrible waste.

Once you start a scene, all your Preparation goes away. It lasts only for the very first moment like a kind of a springboard. Don't hold on to it.

Take your attention off of yourself and put it on the other actors in the scene. Take your hands off your jugs and act!

☙

Bruce Davison (no relation to our friends Crazy Ass Bruce, Bruce the Younger, Bruce from *Beyond Therapy* or Bruce Springsteen, for that matter) is the quintessential Working Actor. He started out as a Nobody and bounced around in the New York Theatre until he landed the lead role in the 1989 film, *Longtime Companion*.

After the movie came out, he never looked back. He works all the fucking time.

A groundbreaking story about the ravages caused by the AIDS epidemic, *Longtime Companion* features a strong ensemble of New York-based actors. Davison gives a standout performance as a gay man who is nursing his dying lover.

It was a tender and effortlessly subtle portrayal, and Davison rightly earned a slew of awards, including the Golden Globe for Best Supporting Actor. Joe Pesci's flashy (and anything but subtle) turn in *Goodfellas* beat Davison out of a richly-deserved Oscar.

In the climactic scene of *Longtime Companion,* Davison gently coaxes his dying sweetheart to let go—to accept the end.

This scene contains a classic emotional trap. The sucker play is to make the scene about *me,* i.e., "my lover is dying; poor, poor pitiful me."

A lesser actor would crank himself up with an over-the-top Preparation and roll around onscreen in his own self-indulgent goo.

Davison doesn't make that mistake. His approach is wonderfully simple. He *takes his attention off of himself and puts it onto his partner.* He calmly gives his boyfriend permission to die. It's one of the most heart-wrenching scenes I've ever seen.

Bruce Davison is the archetypical Working Actor. He's the kind of actor we should all aspire to be.

Davison never became a "movie star," per se. He's been in scores of movies, of course, and movies-of-the-week, too (back in the day when they made those cash cows).

He also starred in a couple of series, including the ludicrous *Harry and the Hendersons,* about a suburban family and their pet Sasquatch. (Oh, TV, your creative genius never ceases to amaze me.)

Mainly, though, Bruce has kicked around, playing supporting movie parts and lots of recurring roles on TV series. He's what's known in the business as an "Industry Name."

That means he's sort of, kind of famous—but not really. People recognize him as, "You know ... uhh ... that guy that was in ... ah, man, I forget its name ... *that show.*"

But the casting people and producers certainly know who Bruce Davison is, because he always delivers. They hire him all the goddamn time.

I had the good luck to work with Bruce on a "piece of shit" TV show. We played members of the Joint Chiefs of Staff involved in a plot to overthrow the President. Naturally, the coup was being led by a pretty girl in a short skirt. (Honest to God.)

It was a great job, though. It shot in Hawaii, which meant First Class air travel and First Class accommodations on Waikiki Beach.

Going on location is the greatest scam in the world. You get a chance to blow town. No bills. No appointments. No chores. All the normal day-to-day bullshit gets left behind. There's only you, your project and restaurant meals paid for out of your per diem.

But the best thing about location is the people.

Freed from the dulling sameness of everyday life, actors can be a pretty lively bunch of people to hang out with. Dinners are shared. Libations are guzzled. Yarns are spun. Friendships are made, albeit transient ones.

Contrary to the Business-Guy-In-Suit roles that he often plays, Bruce Davison is really an old hippie. He's got a million showbiz stories to tell, and he's not shy about sharing them. And he's one of the nicest guys in The Game.

Once, in a rare, quiet moment, I got to ask Bruce about that death scene from *Longtime Companion*.

"It was easy," Davison said. "I helped a family member die once."

I pointed out the obvious emotional trap in the scene.

"Well, yes. I suppose," he continued. "But it's his scene. He's the one who's dying."

Bruce was being modest, in my opinion. What he did wasn't easy at all. He just made it *look* easy.

Bruce confirmed what I have been telling you. *He took his attention off of himself and put it onto his partner.* And he did it in the movie's climactic scene!

In that moment of utter selflessness, Davison exposed his humanity for all the world to see. That takes guts and humility. It also takes tremendous skill.

☙

Sanford Meisner spent forty years of his life teaching actors how to truthfully respond to their partner's behavior. The lynchpin of the Meisner Technique is his famous Repetition Exercise. Here's how it works:

Two actors sit across from each other and make observations about one another.

>Actor 1: You're wearing a blue snood.
>
>Actor 2: I'm wearing a blue snood.
>
>Actor 1: You're wearing a blue snood!
>
>Actor 2: I'm wearing a blue snood.
>
>Actor 1: Snood is a funny word.
>
>Actor 2: Yes, snood is a funny word.

This exercise trains actors to pick up impulses from each other and then improvise spontaneously, based solely upon their partner's behavior.

It is important that Working Actors learn to recognize and act upon that "first" impulse rather than trying to intellectually process it before responding. This exercise takes the brain out of the equation. It requires that we listen and respond to our partner truthfully.

As you develop your own "Method," it wouldn't be a bad idea to find a really good teacher of Meisner technique and to explore Meisner's approach to behavior. Ask around.

In the meantime, here's a variation on an exercise that Yale Dean, Lloyd Richards, ran a group of us through (a million years ago.)

I've embellished it a tad, and have used it in my Studio A lab with very good results. You can use it to train yourself to get out of your head and to sensitize yourself to your partner's behavior. (Or, to put it crassly, to get your hands off your jugs and act.)

This exercise is especially beneficial for actors who don't know each other. It's also a good jumping off point as you approach a new role.

Appropriately, this exercise will require a scene partner.

From an early age, we're all taught that it's not polite to stare at people. We are programmed by our parents not to do it. The result is that, quite often, we don't take the time to really *see* people. We become invisible to one another.

Sit across from your partner and look at him. Look at his face, his hair, his clothes, his shoes, etc. Take five minutes or so and really try to *see* him.

Now close your eyes. See him in your mind's eye. Describe him in detail.

Now, open your eyes. How accurate were you? Did you leave anything out? Did you remember the tiniest of details?

Now, look at your partner and see *something that you love* about him. Take your time.

Here's your line of dialogue:

"I love you."

The impulse to say the line should come from something you see in your partner or something your partner does. Once that impulse comes, say your line. Then, the exercise is complete.

If this exercise is done properly, we've taken two actors who may not know each other at all and, by giving them permission to break societal rules (to look at each other openly) we've helped them to create the beginnings of a truthful, loving relationship within only a few minutes. How cool is that?

Now, try the exercise again.

Look for something in your partner that you hate about him. Or something about him that's suspicious. Or something that terrifies you about him. There are a lot of different possibilities.

Train yourself to place your attention onto your partner.

Now, obviously you're not going to be able to do an exercise like this on a movie set. If, for example, I had asked Julia Roberts if she'd mind if I dropped by her trailer for some "exercise" prior to shooting *Erin Brockovich*, there's a pretty good chance that I'd have been fired within the hour. Nonetheless, once you've trained yourself to work this way, there are real world applications where this exercise can come in quite handy.

Let's say you've won a guest-starring role on a popular TV drama. They've written you a wife. You're supposed to love her. You've done your Preparation. You know what love feels like in your body. Now all you have to do is attach those feelings to her.

Observe her. Find *something specific you love about her.*

It can be her wicked smarts or the way she smiles as she flips her hair past her shoulder. Maybe it's her offbeat sense of humor or her meticulous attention to her nose hair maintenance.

It doesn't matter what it is so long as it's something *specific* about her that strikes your fancy.

Fall in love with that small, even insignificant detail. Then, let your Imagination run amok.

"Oh my god. That throaty laugh! I've gotta have her!"

Just get your attention off of yourself and put it onto your partner.

As a real world example, while rehearsing for my trial scene in Erin Brockovich, I noticed something about Julia Roberts that I found *contemptible.*

Now, don't get me wrong. Julia seemed like a very nice person. She was quite cordial, in fact. But something about the way she held her head kind of bugged me.

I let my Imagination take control.

"Man, look at the way this chick holds her head up. Who does she think she is anyway? The goddamned Queen of England? Well, fuck her and the polo pony she rode in on."

So, I improvised the scene using my specific feelings of contempt. The scene played quite well, because I had a *truthful reaction to my scene partner's behavior.* I rather enjoyed taking her apart on the witness stand.

So let's review:

Don't get stuck in your Preparation. Train yourself to put your attention onto your partner. Find specific impulses to act. Use your Imagination. Improvise the scene truthfully based upon your feelings. Your attention to these details will pay huge dividends.

CHAPTER EIGHT

Improvisation

> *"No, improvising is wonderful.*
> *But, the thing is that you cannot improvise*
> *unless you know exactly what you're doing."*
> —Christopher Walken

Acting—all acting—is improvisation.

There is no such thing as a performance. Everything is a rehearsal, even if the cameras are rolling or there are people in the audience watching us. It's just another run-through, another improvisation.

We define the boundaries of the improvisation using our Imaginations and our Emotional Skill Sets, but every scene remains an improvisation based upon the behavior of our acting partners. We improvise (using the lines as written) within certain, clearly defined parameters.

But we start the work in a place of unknowingness, not knowing what is going on in a scene or what is going to happen in the future.

☙

Bruce Lee (certainly not to be confused with the veritable constellation of other Bruces already celebrated in these pages) was born in San Francisco's Chinatown and raised in Kowloon by his opera singer father and half-Caucasian mother. They named him Lee Jun-fan (literally "Return Again") but, it is said, the doctor who delivered him was the one who called him "Bruce."

In 1959, 18-year-old Bruce Lee did return to San Francisco, sent by his parents to live with his sister because of his academic misadventures and, not surprisingly, for his street fighting. Soon, however, Bruce found himself working as a waiter in Seattle while he completed his high school education.

After graduating, Bruce entered the University of Washington. He would say later that he had been a Philosophy major, but University records (while confirming that he did indeed study Philosophy) list him as a Drama major.

In 1964, Bruce Lee dropped out of school, moved to Oakland and opened a martial arts studio.

Later that year, at the Long Beach International Karate Championships, Lee was spotted by TV producer (and sometime actor) William Dozier and was asked to audition for a pilot. Lee won the part, but the show went nowhere.

The following year, Lee was cast as Kato in the short-lived series, *The Green Hornet.*

After the series failed, Lee kicked around in Hollywood doing small TV parts and choreographing fights for films. He taught martial arts and had some famous clients including Steve McQueen, James Coburn, Lee Marvin and Kareem Abdul-Jabbar.

Lee pitched a series idea that Warner Bros. (arguably) stole from him and turned into the hit show, *Kung Fu* with David Carradine, a non-Asian, non-martial artist.

Soon after, Lee returned home to Hong Kong in hopes of making a film he could showcase to Hollywood execs. The enormous financial successes of *The Big Boss* (1971) and *Fist of Fury* (1972) across Asia led to stardom for Lee.

The Way of the Dragon (which also introduced the world to Chuck Norris) soon followed, and, in 1973, Warner Bros. co-produced Lee's next film, *Enter the Dragon*. Bruce Lee was well on his way.

Six days before *Enter the Dragon* came out, Lee complained of a headache, took a painkiller and went down for a nap. Sadly, he never woke up. He was only thirty-three years old.

In 1999, Bruce Lee was included in Time Magazine's list of the "100 Most Influential People of the 20th Century."

That's certainly remarkable, especially considering that his IMDb credits reflect a grand total of five films and a mere handful of TV shows (including such forgettable "pieces of shit" as *Blondie* and *Here Come the Brides*).

Dying young is awesome publicity, but I recommend against it as a career path.

Lee's parents had introduced their son to martial arts instruction when he was 13 so that he might better defend himself. Hong Kong was a pretty rough town at the time, and Bruce kept running up against the wrong guys.

Bruce's Dad taught him the basics of Wu-style T'ai Chi Ch'uan before Bruce graduated to formal training in Wing Chun. Eventually, he would study not only Tam Toi but western-style boxing and epee fencing, as well.

So after *The Green Hornet* was canceled, Lee opened the Jun Fan Institute of Gung Fu.

Convinced that formal techniques were not useful in the disorganized arena of street fighting, Lee developed his own philosophy and combat system. He called it Jeet Kune Do, literally "Way of the Intercepting Fist." Lee described Jeet Kune Do as "the style of no style."

Unlike traditional martial arts disciplines, Jeet Kune Do emphasized speed, and rejected classical form. Lee believed in explosive attacks that minimized telegraphing the attacker's intentions.

Lee taught situational fighting, training his followers how best to react to different sorts of attacks. (Basically, Improvisation for fighters.)

Lee was also an early adapter of good nutrition, cardio work and weight training. (Necessities not just for the jock athlete but for the Working Actor athlete as well.) Most importantly, Lee sought the fastest, most efficient way possible to win any confrontation.

The style of no style.

Lee's approach was an eclectic, winnowing down process. He employed techniques he had learned from many disciplines, "casting off what is useless."

"I have not," Lee said, "invented a 'new style,' composite, modified or otherwise, that is set within distinct form as apart from 'this' method or 'that' method. On the contrary, I hope to free my followers from clinging to styles, patterns or molds ..."

Try many things. Cast off what is useless.

Bruce Lee emphasized the Work Ethic of learning many different disciplines fully, discarding what didn't work and, in his words, "absorbing what is useful."

Dig deep. Absorb what is useful.

Along your journey towards becoming a Working Actor, it would certainly be beneficial to apply Lee's approach to your continuing education. As you move from studio to studio, from show to show, from job to job, absorb "what is useful" and toss the rest.

Steal what works for you, and create your own approach, your own Method.

"Jeet Kune Do," Lee once said, "is just a name used, a boat to get one across, and once across it is to be discarded and not carried on one's back."

To Bruce Lee, even his own philosophy was disposable.

☙

Bruce Lee amassed a huge library and read voraciously. (Something you should consider.) Though an atheist, Lee's philosophy was heavily influenced by Taoist and Buddhist teachings.

In a rare TV interview he did in Hong Kong, Lee said:

"Be like water ... Empty your mind, be formless. Shapeless like water. If you put water into a cup, it becomes the cup. You put water into a bottle and it becomes the bottle. You put it in a teapot, it becomes the teapot. Now, water can flow or it can crash. Be water, my friend."[7]

Be water. Start neutral.

Water is neutral. It's flavorless and colorless.

In a lake, water can be still. In a river, it can flow. In the ocean, it can roar.

In a scene, you are water. You can flow or you can crash—or you can do any of the myriad things that we humans do in the course of our transactions.

Defining the dimensions of your teapot allows you to improvise the moments based upon the behavior of your acting partners. You are *alive* inside—fluid and ready to respond to whatever your partner throws your way.

☙

The following is a scene I wrote for the actors in my Studio A lab. I instructed them to go off in a corner with their partners and learn the lines mechanically. No "acting."

>   Actor 1: Where have you been?
>
>   Actor 2: It's been a long time.
>
>   Actor 1: You don't look so good.
>
>   Actor 2: It's hard.
>
>   Actor 1: Did you find him?
>
>   Actor 2: I'm close.
>
>   Actor 1: What about us?
>
>   Actor 2: It's okay. Don't worry.

Now, get a partner. Divide up the parts and try it. Sit together and learn the lines. For the sake of the exercise, the lines should be read with about as much emphasis as this:

Actor 1: Blah blah blah blah?

Actor 2: Blah blah blah blah blah.

Continue to work on it by rote until you have both thoroughly learned all eight lines in the scene.

So, what's this *Scene With No Name* about? Go back and re-read it. What's it about?

When I asked the actors in Studio A this question, they were very eager to jump in with an answer. In spite of the fact that I had told them to just learn the lines by rote, their brains had already begun to formulate this collection of phrases into a scene.

So, what's it about?

It's a trick question. The only possible answer is: "I don't know."

We can't possibly know what the scene is about until we've worked on it. Until then, it isn't about anything. It's just a page with bunch of words on it.

Go back and read the scene again. It's utter nonsense. It's not a scene until we actors have defined the parameters of our Improvisation and have turned it into a scene.

Start from a place of unknowingness.

We're all so anxious to jump in and *act*. We burn to roll the words around in our mouths. We want to *feel* stuff, and we want to *do* stuff. We want to leap right to the ending. We want to *act our fucking asses off*.

Why? Because it feels good.

Problem is, it's bullshit. That's what amateurs do, and some pros, too. Mediocre ones. They're what Meisner derisively called "Line Actors."

Until his death, Meisner insisted that Laurence Olivier wasn't a great actor. Why? Because he felt that Olivier was a Line Actor of the highest order. From his point of view, Olivier sucked.

While that point might be argued, go back and watch a few Olivier films and you might see what Meisner was driving at even if you don't agree. Regardless, it's pretty clear that Olivier was certainly very old school and that his style was very different from what Meisner was teaching American actors.

You want to turn pro. You want to have a career that will earn you a decent living and span a lifetime. You want to kick the bucket in the make-up chair on your 98th birthday.

The best place to start that journey is with the understanding that the lines—all lines—mean nothing at all. The lines have no value until we Working Actors give them value.

Start from a place of unknowingness.

Be water. Start neutral. Learn the dialogue by rote, giving it no inflection—no flavor—whatsoever. The lines don't mean anything at all. You want them to just fall out of you.

A couple of the actors in Studio A struggled with this practice.

It's not easy, but give it a try. This process will slow you down. It will keep you from jumping to easy line readings and from making shallow "choices."

Be brave.

Have the courage to start your work from that place of unknowingness. It is okay, preferable even, that you don't know what the scene is about or what is going to happen.

Begin every Improvisation, take on every part, without preconceived notions. It's a "piece of shit." It's just a bunch of words strung together.

Start neutral. Be water.

Kicking ass will come later.

CHAPTER NINE

Given Circumstances

"The role of the artist is to ask questions, not answer them."
—Anton Chekhov

Okay, so I am water. Now what? Now it's time to give form to my teapot.

Lucky me! I've just won the much sought-after role of ACTOR 1 in the glamorous and brilliant play, *Scene with No Name,* by the overrated dramatist, Pat Skipper. It's my job to improvise the part.

Where do I begin to define the parameters of the improvisation? How do I give shape to my water?

I'll start (as Stella Adler would want me to) with the Given Circumstances of the scene. I'll ask myself questions, then—

I'll let my Imagination do the rest of the work.

Robert Lewis was long gone by the time I got to Yale. When Robert Brustein abandoned Yale for Harvard in 1979, Lloyd Richards became Dean of the Drama School.

An older man who cut a courtly figure, Richards, in addition to his duties at the school, was in charge of the Yale Repertory Theatre as well as Artistic Director of the prestigious Eugene O'Neill National Playwrights Conference.

Richards wasn't around school much and, to my 21-year-old self, he seemed ancient and hopelessly out of touch. (I was, as I may have mentioned previously, a young asshole.)

Richards lured Earle Gister away from Carnegie Mellon to become Associate Dean and Chair of the Yale School of Drama MFA Acting Program. Gister ran the school.

A wiry little guy with coarse salt-and-pepper hair who forever peered over the top of the half-moon spectacles that seemed permanently super-glued to his nose, Earle was ardent, insightful and somewhat dogged in the classroom.

He taught scores of Working Actors how to act. Both Robert Foxworth and Judith Light studied under him at Carnegie.

At Yale, Earle taught Frances McDormand, Jane Kaczmarek, Angela Bassett, Charles Dutton, John Turturro, Patricia Clarkson, Courtney Vance, Paul Giamatti and Liev Schreiber, to name but a few of the hundreds of Working Actors who passed through the doors of his studio.

One of my colleagues once told me, "I never learned anything in acting class—except of course from Earle."

☙

One time, I ran into Gister at an alumni cocktail party.

By this time, his nicotine habit had caused him to lose his vocal cords to cancer, and he had to lug around an electrolarynx—one of those vibrator deals that the patient shoves up against his neck that allows him to create an approximation of speech. It was freaky and I'm sure it frustrated him no end, but it didn't diminish his impish spirit in the least.

"You live in my head, Earle," I said. "I can't pick up a scene without hearing your voice saying, 'Who am I? What do I want?'"

Gister was vastly amused.

There's a book floating around called *The Gister Method*. Yep, that's right. Yet *another* Method.

Written in conjunction with a fawning graduate student, Gister's book is painfully pedantic and as dry as a Mastodon's dick.

It's a reminder that, in addition to being a great acting teacher, Earle was first and foremost a college professor. He spent his entire career surrounded by academics—people who like books that are neat, orderly, footnote [8] and without fucking cuss words.

Therefore, it's not surprising that *The Gister Method* is dull as dirt. (There is a section, I kid you not, on how to take notes in your script.)

Still, I [halfheartedly] recommend the book to all hardcore university acting theorists and fully recommend it for insomniacs across the globe. Earle's ideas are in there, and I guess it beats the hell out of his not having a book at all.

Let's take Bruce Lee's advice on this one. Let's absorb what is useful and cast off what isn't.

The most helpful thing that Earle taught was his approach to Given Circumstances. He would ask his students two simple questions, and he would ask them over and over again until we could hear him in our sleep.

Who am I? What do I want?

༄

Let's leave aside, "What do I want?" for another chapter and focus on "Who am I?"

Here's the description of a character I once played on a TV show:

"[GENERAL WOODLAND] 50s. This high-ranking Air Force General is also privy to the conspiracy. However, he is hesitant about the treasonous plan that is in the offing. His reluctance to participate gets him killed. GUEST STAR."

There's not much to go on. He's a reluctant General who gets killed. (He's also a Guest Star, meaning my lifelong ambition of becoming a wealthy TV Star is once again foiled. Curses.)

I need to work on my Given Circumstances.

I start neutral. I read the script. Not a lot of help there. Just a bunch of meaningless dialogue about some coup.

Basically, I'm right back where I started—in a place of unknowingness. I still don't know dick about this guy.

But if I ask myself the question, "Who am I?" and let my Imagination run with the ball, maybe I'll find something that will inform my behavior. Maybe my Imagination will lead me to a place of knowledge.

Who am I?

I'm 55 and I'm on the Joint Chiefs of Staff. I grew up a military brat. I attended the Air Force Academy and received a Masters from George Washington University. I served all over the goddamned world including Germany and in assorted hellholes like the Philippines. I like to party. I enjoy an occasional whore. I've been married for 32 years. She thinks I drink too much, but fuck her. What does she know? We have two kids in college, a boy at Columbia and a girl at Duke Medical School.

So, which is the better character description?

The second one, obviously. It took me about five minutes to dream it up. Is there anything I can play with using this information? You bet your ass.

If the plot fails, we will all be executed. What will happen to my kids then? Even if we succeed, what kind of world will they grow up in?

Now I have a specific reason for my evil General's reluctance to go through with the coup. In fact, maybe I'm not such a bad dude after all. Maybe I'm just a guy in a tough situation.

See what I've done here? I've humanized the guy. I'm no longer a cardboard cutout TV villain. I'm a living, breathing human being with hopes and dreams and fears.

That's why we work this way. We want to bring this shit to life!

Next, I might find the need to have a drink—you know, just a small one to steady the nerves, and then maybe one or two or six more.

Now, I've established some *behavior*, something for me to be doing during my scenes.

What we're looking for is information that will inform our behavior.

I once knew a young actress who would obsessively scribble down complicated autobiographies in spiral notebooks. It seemed like overkill to me, but it worked for her. Try it out. If it'll help you get somewhere, write to your heart's content.

While preparing for my star turn in *Scene with No Name,* here are some questions that I need to ask myself:

Who am I?

How old am I? Where did I grow up? Where do I live? What do I do for a living? How much money do I make? What kind of car do I drive?

Am I married? Divorced? Dating somebody? Single? Do I have kids? How many? Do they live with me?

If I'm divorced, what happened? If I'm single, why? If I'm dating someone, who is she?

What are my politics? What is my religion (or lack thereof)? Etc.

So, now that I've answered most of these questions, am I ready to act the crap out of the glamorous part of ACTOR 1 in the blockbuster *Scene with No Name*?

No. Not quite. Remember, there's someone else in the scene with me. I've got a few more questions to ask.

Who are they?

Are we in the same family? Are we married? For how long? Are we friends? For how long? Lovers? For how long? Acquaintances? Strangers?

When did I see ACTOR 2 last? What happened the last time we saw each other? How do I feel about ACTOR 2? Do I love him? Hate him?

I was once on a show called *Boston Public,* one of several David E. Kelley shows that I've gotten to act in. Kelley's something of an odd duck.

A quiet, under-the-radar sort of person, Kelley eschews a writing staff. He prefers to pen almost all the scripts for his shows himself, in longhand on yellow legal pads. On top of that, he rarely rewrites. How he does it is a complete mystery. But he's spooky good.

Kelley worked for Steven Bochco on *Doogie Howser, M.D.* and *L.A. Law.* He wrote and produced *The Practice, Ally McBeal* and *Boston Legal.* He is a hit-making machine AND he gets to go home to Michelle Pfeiffer at the end of a long day. Sucks to be him.

Boston Public is set in a public high school. In my first scene, my wife and I get called into the principal's office. We don't know why. The man informs us that our daughter is claiming that she has been sexually abused by her teacher.

The Principal is obviously expecting a shit storm. Instead, we awkwardly tell him that our daughter is in counseling for mental health issues and that she's made similar charges in the past.

It was a peculiar scene that, in the playing of it, felt weirdly flat. It wasn't working. Desperate, I quickly started asking questions.

Who am I?

I'm a guy who just got pulled out of an important meeting to come to my daughter's school.

Who are they?

I love my daughter, but she's doing batshit crazy stuff. Again. I wish she had a better Mother. This is all her Mother's fault.

Eureka!

I turned to the talented Working Actress who was playing the Mom, and said, "How do you think this marriage is going?" She nodded. "Not too good."

Now we had a scene to play.

The situation no longer had anything to do with our daughter (who wasn't even in the scene). It was all about our crumbling marriage. We blamed each other. We took out the stress of the situation on one other.

There was now a ton of stuff to play.

Was it in the script? No. With apologies to David Kelley, the script was just a jumble of words.

Did the scene work? Hell, yes. Did David Kelley intend for it to go that way? Who knows? Who cares? It was full of *life*.

☙

In Studio A, two young actresses were working on my brilliant *Scene with No Name*.

I asked the other actors in the room for a relationship for them to play. The class decided that they should be sisters who haven't seen each other for two years. I asked for a location. Someone suggested the backyard.

Obviously, "sisters" is a very general "Who Am I?" We need to delve in more deeply, ask some questions:

Who's the oldest? Why haven't we seen each other for so long? Whose fault is that? How long have I lived in this house? Is this our childhood home? Where am I coming from? Do I live there? What did she do to me? Etc.

Remember, you're looking for stuff that will *inform your behavior*.

For instance, in the *Scene with No Name,* ACTOR 1 asks, "Did you find him?"

While establishing our Given Circumstances (the "Who am I?") we must ask the question, "Who is *he*?"

Is he our Dad, our long-lost brother or a shared former lover? Obviously, knowing those circumstances will *inform our behavior*.

The more specific you are with your answer to questions such as these, the better.

Here's another valuable question worth asking:

Who are they to me?

Another day in Studio A, a pair was working on Noel Coward's *Private Lives.*

Amanda is at a honeymoon resort with her new husband, Victor. She's just seen her former husband, Elyot. He's also a guest at the hotel. Understandably, Amanda freaks out.

The woman playing Amanda was struggling to find the truth of this broadly comic scene. She was working double-time, trying to be funny. I stopped her.

"Who is Elyot?" I asked.

"My ex-husband," she replied impatiently, thinking me a fool.

"No, no. To you. In your own life, who is *your* Elyot?"

Almost every adult woman has an Elyot in her past, some former flame who, in spite of her current situation, could waltz right back in and fuck up everything. Elyot's a bad boy and he has a lot of power.

The actress had an immediate emotional reaction. Her complexion darkened, as crosscurrents of fear, lust and hatred boiled up inside her.

Answering that question with specificity, casting someone from her personal life to play Elyot, *informed her behavior*. Amanda's desperate desire to leave the resort suddenly became very real to her. And the scene played. It was funny.

♋

Now that I've established the Given Circumstances, am I ready to act the *Scene with No Name* now? Almost. ("Oh, Dude! This is like work. Can't I just get discovered?")

The most important moment in any scene you'll ever play is the moment before the scene starts.

I need to work on my Preparation. I need to establish what's happening in the moments before I start talking. Then, and only then, am I ready to have a go at it.

In Studio A, based on the specific Given Circumstances we worked up for the *Scene with No Name* (the "Who am I?"), I told ACTOR 2 to find an activity to work on in her backyard.

She started planting annuals.

As part of her Imaginary Circumstances, I suggested to ACTOR 2 that it was *"as-if" the backyard were her Zen place.*

That helped her establish her territory. This was *her* home, and it put her in a position of power.

As ACTOR 2 began to work on her Preparation, we observed her relaxing into the reality of the scene she was creating. Concentrating on her new little flowers, she made her own little Nirvana.

For ACTOR 1, we devised a completely differently Preparation using Imaginary Circumstances.

I told her to grab her purse and her keys. I told her that it was *"as-if" she had been driving for ten hours straight with only one stop for gas and one lousy bathroom break.* She had just pulled up at her sister's house.

ACTOR 1 knocks on the front door. No one answers. She continues knocking, then banging and then pounding on the door. Minutes pass. Finally, she crosses around to the back of the house.

ACTOR 1 enters the backyard frustrated to the point of tears, her hand throbbing. She observes her sister off in her own little world, humming.

Now, they had a scene they could play.

The words are just words until we invest them with value.

In this particular instance, the triumphant *Scene with No Name* was being acted by two women, but it could just as easily have been played by men. It also could have been played by a male-female couple.

The characters could have been lovers or co-workers or farmer cousins shoveling steaming dung out of a barn. It doesn't matter.

Also, the conflict could have been about anything, depending upon the "Who Am I?" and the Preparation.

Without us working on it, the *Scene with No Name* lacks meaning. The words lack significance. It's water without a teapot.

To illustrate this point, I had the two women switch Preparations in the scene.

ACTOR 1 was now planting flowers and zoning out. ACTOR 2 entered after a long road trip and banged on the door for five minutes.

The lines they spoke were exactly the same as in the first run-through, but the new scene they improvised still played. The Improvisation played out differently (as the balance of power had shifted due to the change in their Preparations) but the scene still made perfect sense. Why? Because the "Who Am I?" and the Preparation were so strong.

The lines are just words. They're formless. We give them meaning.

Notice that I gave both Actors physical things to hold onto in their scene.

ACTOR 1 is carrying her keys and purse. ACTOR 2 has plants and gardening supplies (even if they're partially mimed).

Why did I do this?

Props, clothing, furniture and activities keep the actor grounded in the physical reality of the scene. They're our lifeblood.

Besides being visually stimulating for the viewer, this "business" provides us actors with secondary points of concentration that allow us to remain anchored in space.

More importantly, they help to create a more *immersive acting experience*. (A subject for a later chapter.)

I once played a dull as dirt conference room scene on the TV show, *Mad Men*.

Lucky for me, the helpful Prop Master had provided us half-dozen actors with coffee cups, plates, knives, napkins and a big honking Danish. Suddenly, a very unremarkable scene became quite interesting for me to play.

I drank. I chewed. I talked with my mouth full. When the goo got stuck in my teeth, I went with it. I was immersed in the experience of the scene.

Wouldn't you know it? I was the only actor in the scene who took so much as a sip of coffee from the bounty of potential behavior the crew had provided for us.

Who do you think won that scene?

As Meisner once said, "An ounce of behavior is worth a pound of words."

☙

Here's a very cool exercise for you to try. I stole the idea from Kate McGregor-Stewart and adapted it for my own Studio.

Get a partner. Go to the library or a bookstore. Each of you should select separate plays written by different authors.

Both actors then choose a scene from their play. It doesn't matter which scene—with one caveat. Pick scenes that have relatively short lines, a few sentences each.

Each of you should choose a character to play from your script. It doesn't matter which character. Agree on the number of lines you're both going to learn from your script, say twelve-to-fifteen lines.

At this point, you should separately take your scripts and learn the lines from your play on your own. Again, learn the lines by rote. No acting. No inflection. Start neutral.

Meet up and work on the lines. Sit opposite from each other and say the lines. Say them mechanically until you have them down.

As an example, here's a very short scene I cobbled together from *The Caretaker* by Harold Pinter and *Come Blow Your Horn* by Neil Simon.

COME BLOW THE CARETAKER

by Harold Simon

HAROLD: [DIALOGUE REDACTED BY MY ATTORNEY.]

SIMON: [DIALOGUE REDACTED BY MY OTHER ATTORNEY.]

HAROLD: [DIALOGUE REDACTED BY MY ATTORNEY'S PARALEGAL.]

SIMON: [DIALOGUE REDACTED BY THE PARALEGAL'S THIRD COUSIN.]

HAROLD: [DIALOGUE EATEN BY THE PARALEGAL'S THIRD COUSIN'S DOG.]

What's this scene about? The obvious answer is "nothing."

Pinter and Simon were two of the more successful playwrights of the 20th Century, but I've made a complete hash of their work (purely for academic purposes, mind you. So don't fucking sue me). I've cribbed some lines from each and have mashed-up a new and utterly meaningless scene.

It's up to us as Working Actors to provide the meaning by engaging our Imaginations to create the "Who am I?" and a truthful Preparation.

Create the teapot.

Now that you and your partner know the words to your scene, take a few minutes and ask yourselves these questions: "Who am I?" and "Who are they?" Let your imaginations run wild.

Then, pick a location.

Now, separately take a few minutes to work up a Preparation for this hybrid scene.

Finally, improvise the scene using the lines as written. End of exercise.

You can also do variations on this exercise if it suits you. Change your "Who am I?" and try it again. Exchange Preparations.

Think of it as a trip to the gym. You're Athletes, and it's a good, rugged workout.

In Studio A, we spent countless hours doing scenes this way.

Why? Because working like this confounds expectations. It removes intellect from the equation. It forces the Athlete in us to improvise based upon the behavior of our scene partners without preconceived notions.

It also helps us avoid the pedestrian, clichéd and uninspired "choices" that the uninventive ego would make if left to its own boring devices.

If, for instance, I were given a part in Sam Shepard's *True West*, my brain may very well jump to certain imagination-killing conclusions. I may start to act "in the style of" Sam Shepard. I may remember the movie version with John Malkovich and start "acting like" Malkovich.

If, however, my scene partner is answering my Shepard lines with words from Edward Albee's *Who's Afraid of Virginia Woolf?*, it blows those expectations out the water, freeing the Athlete in me to improvise truthfully based upon my partner's behavior.

My brain can't get in the way.

Remember, you're simply using your Imagination to define the parameters of the improvisation, to create your teapot.

Inside the pot, you're fluid. You can flow or you can crash. You can be still or you can rage like a storm.

But you begin the journey as water, in a place of unknowingness. By asking these questions, you invite your Imagination, not your intellect, to guide you to knowledge.

CHAPTER TEN

What's My Motivation?

> *"When an actor comes to me and wants to discuss his character, I say, 'It's in the script.' If he says, 'But what's my motivation?,' I say, 'Your salary.'"*
> —Alfred Hitchcock

In the previous chapter, Earle Gister's helpful "Who am I?" approach to establishing Given Circumstances got us out of our heads and up on to our feet to improvise some scenes. But how do we translate all that hard work we did into *Action*?

Let's consider the second of Earle's famous questions:

"What am I doing?"

In *The Gister Method*, there are lengthy sections about Objectives and Super-Objectives, Actions, Intentions, Motivations and Obstacles. In acting classes across the country, you'll hear these words get tossed around like a Caesar salad. They're often used interchangeably.

"What's my motivation?" has become a punchline on fucking sitcoms, for God's sake.

These days, everybody but everybody in every acting school in America is teaching "intention."

"What's your intention?" "Find your intention?" "Show me your intention." Teachers may even disguise the same talk by telling us to "pick a specific verb."

"Hey, what's your verb?" "Tell us your verb." "No wonder you sucked. You picked the wrong verb!"

In his book, Earle includes a mega-list of action words. And he's not the only one.

I've plowed through several acting books lately with virtually identical lists of crap that the authors have culled from the dictionary.

Here's a small sample:

To cajole, to accuse, to flirt, to seduce, to stalk, to punch, to ... please give me a fucking break.

There's even a paperback called *Actions, The Actors Thesaurus* (by Caldarone and Lloyd-Williams) that's filled with verbs, verbs and more verbs. That's the whole fucking book! It's a list of verbs! (What a joke. Wish I'd thought of it.)

I get why this has happened, though. Intention is easy to teach. It doesn't require one ounce of creativity. It's easily quantifiable and easy to grade. ("Dear Mrs. Skipper, Pat got a B-Minus in Acting this semester because his verb choices simply were not up to the standards of this fine institution.")

Here's how it goes in these academic acting programs:

You sit down with your script. You engage your intellect. You break down your scenes into "beats" (or "bits" if you've got a Russian accent). You pop open your thesaurus and choose an action verb for each section. And, "look, Ma! I'm acting!"

If you're a really, really good student, you can rewrite every single line of text in your own words. And if you want extra credit, you can pencil your subtext into the margins. ("I'm saying yes, but I really mean no! Damn, I'm smart!")

Look, it's all bullshit. Up until this point in this book, we've worked hard to get ourselves *out* of our heads. "Choosing" verbs and intentions is an intellectual exercise. This crap just blocks the Imagination. It turns the Athlete into a fucking bookworm.

I say to hell with all that noise. It's amateur night. It's useless. Let's cast it off.

∽

Aristotle said that, in the end, all people want happiness. Everything we strive for, be it money, power, sex or love, we seek because *we think that the thing we pursue will make us happy.*

When preparing for a role, simply ask this question:

What will make me happy?

Instead of rummaging around in your *Funk and Wagnalls*, using your brain to "choose" a verb out of left field, the question, "What will make me happy?" will engage your Imagination.

"What will make me happy?" will open up a new frontier of exciting, fresh possibilities.

There are people who strive for justice, wealth or freedom in their quest for happiness. Others seek power, fame or inner peace.

There's love. There's sex. People derive happiness from their families and their places of worship. For many, happiness is a goal in and of itself.

Of course, some folks pursue their happiness in more peculiar ways. There's some freaky shit out there on the Net. Stygiophiliacs get sexually excited by thoughts of Hell and damnation. Nebulophiliacs get turned on by fog. There are people who are into Formicophilia, sex with insects. (I don't even want to ponder how that *Bug's Life* works.)

As a Working Actor, I have portrayed many "unusual" people. I've made a living playing sociopaths and psychopaths. I've played serial killers, sex offenders and rapists. Because I'm Southern (and because Hollywood has so little imagination) I've been a racist more times than I care to count.

What makes characters like these "happy" can be very complex. By asking the question, I open myself up to all sorts of intriguing possibilities.

The answers lie in the Imagination, not in the intellect.

So, let's be brave. Let's be creative. Let's ask the question.

"What will make me happy?"

Sam Delacroix, the drunken, washed-up actor I played in the Amazon Studios show, *Bosch*, was the sickest fuck I have ever played.

The writing was fantastic and I was thrilled to play it, but being Sam cost me a chunk of my soul.

Here's Sam's story:

As my acting career disintegrates, I climb deeper and deeper into the bottle. Sick of being knocked around by me, my bitch of a wife runs away, leaving me with two young children. At this point, I begin sleeping with my own 12 year-old daughter, Sheila.

Understandably fucked up by all this, Sheila takes out her frustrations on her younger brother, Arthur. She beats him mercilessly over a long period of time. Then Arthur disappears. Convinced that Sheila has killed Arthur, I don't report my son's disappearance to the cops.

CUT TO:

Twenty years later. The boy's body is discovered in a shallow grave. The cops come to me. I confess to the murder in order to protect Sheila.

That's the fucking story. Sweet guy, huh?

So I get to work.

I start neutral. I read the script. I study my words. I read the book the episode is based upon, *City of Bones* by Michael Connelly. I put my Imagination to work answering my questions: Who Am I? Who are they? Who are they *to me?*

I come up with a lot of useable stuff. Now it's time to ask:

What will make me happy?

Great question.

To fuck a kid? To die of alcoholism?

Not too useful. Nah, guess not.

Of course, most actors would answer: *to protect Sheila*. I mean, it's right there in the story, right? "Awesome. Got it. Moving on. Damn, I rock!"

Except ... that's exactly the kind of answer you get if you crack open your thesaurus.

And, guess what? It's the sucker play. Virtually every actor in town can come up with a "motivation" like "to protect." It's bullshit. That's just the fucking plot.

Okay. So *to protect* isn't my answer. I'm back to a place of unknowingness. I'm in the dark.

But then I remember something I read in *City of Bones*. The lines have nothing to do with my character, but they're stuck in my head for some reason. I look them up:

> "'Someone once told me that life was the pursuit of one thing. Redemption. The search for redemption.'
>
> 'For what?'
>
> 'For everything. Anything. We all want to be forgiven.'" [9]

Forgiveness. Redemption. Now I'm getting somewhere.

I'm the most selfish fuck on the planet. I don't want to protect anyone. I want something for *me*. I want someone to forgive me.

But who? My daughter? No. She won't even speak to me. Hasn't for years. Bosch, maybe? The cop I'm confessing to?

Okay, so I'm confessing to Bosch. Does that make him my priest? That's a cool idea. At this point, I go back to my notes. Under, "Who are they?" I write, "Bosch is my priest."

But can Bosch forgive me? That doesn't sound right.

Then, I hear a quote ring out in my head:

"Forgive me my foul murder? That cannot be since I am still possess'd of those effects for which I did the murder ..."

That's Claudius from Hamlet, Act III Scene 3. Where the fuck did that come from?

So, no. Forgiveness is not the answer. I'm lost again. What can a priest give me? Redemption? What does that even mean? Redeemed by whom? To what end?

So I look up Claudius's whole speech and I see this:

> "What if this cursed hand
> Were thicker than itself with brother's blood,
> Is there not rain enough in the sweet heavens
> To wash it white as snow?"

And there's my answer. I want him to absolve me. To baptize me. *To wash me white as snow.* That's the only thing that can bring me any kind of happiness.

By removing my intellect from the equation and engaging my Imagination, I have created a set of Given Circumstances that finally have led me to a playable Action.

To wash me white as snow is an unusual Action phrase, to be sure. (I'm sure the academics would have a field day.) But it played like gangbusters when we shot it.

When approaching a part, create a strong set of Given Circumstances and let your Imagination lead you to a playable Action.

Don't ask, "What's my motivation?" and start scribbling down clichés. Leave that for the hacks.

Ask yourself this: What will make me happy? And let your Imagination be your guide. It'll lead you to more interesting, more playable Actions.

CHAPTER ELEVEN

Making Choices

> *"Clear thinking at the wrong moment can stifle creativity."*
> —Karl Lagerfeld

Here's my opinion on "making choices." Don't. Ask questions.

So, you were cast in the blockbuster *Scene with No Name*. You started neutral, in a place of unknowingness. You learned your words. You created your Given Circumstances by asking, "Who am I?" and "What will make me happy?"

You successfully engaged your Imagination. You found an inspired and playable Action. You worked up a Preparation. You improvised the scene based upon the behavior of your scene partner, and you were fucking brilliant. Kudos.

So where in this process were the infamous "choices" that you were supposed to be making? You know, those "choices" that you've heard so much about in acting class?

They're nowhere to be found, of course, because you didn't make any "choices." You used your Imagination instead.

Look, "making choices" is intellectual. Planning will interfere with your Imagination and get in the way of your athletic abilities.

"Making choices" is limiting. "Making choices" is confining. "Making choices" is useless. Let's cast off "making choices."

Strive to awaken the Athlete inside of you. Ask questions. Allow your Imagination to guide you. Asking questions will open you up to a wealth of athletic possibilities.

Don't plan. Don't "make choices." Ask questions. Create. Adapt. Fight. Win.

༄

Get a bunch of actors into a room and ask them what the goal of the *Artist* is, and you'll get a plethora of responses: to uplift, to shock, to provoke, to entertain, to amaze, to inspire, to exalt, to inform, to enrage, to exhilarate, to thrill and on and on. Given a few hours, actors will come up with a laundry list of fancy phrases to describe their Art. What you won't get at the end of what would likely be a very long and unbearably tedious day is much agreement about what the goal of the Artist is.

George Bernard Shaw may have said it best:

"The goal of an artist is to create the Definitive Work that cannot be surpassed."

Sounds good to me. Who am I to argue with George Fucking Bernard Fucking Shaw, anyway?

But, let's leave that discussion to the never-ending army of dissertation writers. Who gives a rat's ass about Artists? We're Athletes.

What's our goal? What's the *Athlete's* goal?

Well, that's pretty obvious, right?

To win.

For the ballplayer, the goal is clear. Hit, score runs, win games, defeat the competition in the playoffs, win the World Series and slip on the gaudy ring they give you at the end.

The most testosterone-driven men on the planet spend their entire lives developing their Fundamentals and sharpening their Skill Sets, pushing themselves to the limit of their endurance, physically and mentally, in order to beat other hairy-assed dudes out of some shiny diamond jewelry.

Of course, the bling is merely a symbol that marks them forever as champions. Everything that goes along with winning—the money, the endorsement deals, the cars, the chicks, the tacky McMansions—all of it is secondary to winning. Most of them would probably play for beer money if that were the deal. They were born to compete. Fighting to win defines who they are.

Guess what?

Working Actors fight to win, too.

☙

In his book *Audition,* Casting Director Michael Shurtleff says that every scene ever written between two men or two women is a competition.

I would go so far as to say that *every* scene worth playing is a competition—including scenes between men and women. If we run up against a scene that *isn't* a competition, we should turn it into one. At least we'll have something to fight for.

Virtually every scene ever written comes down to one of these options:

> "I'm right, you're wrong."

> "I'm prettier/smarter/stronger/funnier/have a bigger dick than you."

> "I have something you want and I'm not going to give it to you."

> "You have something I desperately need and I'm going to get it from you."

> "'I want love from you.' 'Yeah? Well, I want love from you, but I'm not giving it to you unconditionally.'"

> "We want the same thing, but let's do it my way. Your way sucks."

Whatever the problem is, we fight to win. It's as true in comedy as it is in drama. The only difference is that in comedy we fight over stupid, insignificant minutiae—but we will still fight to the death. In the process, we make ourselves look ridiculously human.

Take a half hour and check out an old *Seinfeld* episode. The show doesn't hold up that well, of course, but study Jason Alexander. He may be the best, and most honest, comic actor you'll ever see.

He fights like crazy to win every scene he's in. That is even more significant considering that the show, as they constantly remind the audience, is about "nothing."

Fights are unpredictable. "Choices" are boring. Fights are messy. Planning is dull. Cool shit happens when we fight.

༄

In the previous chapter, I detailed my creative explorations while I was playing the incestuous, alcoholic child molester, Sam Delacroix, in the Amazon Prime series, *Bosch*.

After I finished celebrating winning the role, I got to work. I started my journey in neutral, in a place of unknowingness. I learned my words. To create my Given Circumstances I began to ask my questions, "Who am I?" and "What will make me happy?" My Imagination finally led me to the playable Action, *"I want him to wash me white as snow."*

Awesome! I'm ready to kick some ass now!

Not quite. (Sorry!)

Now, we've come to the fifth and final question we need to ask ourselves when we're working up our Given Circumstances:

What is my problem?

In every scene we'll ever play, we face a problem. That problem comes in the form of our scene partners. It's all well and good that our Imaginations have led us to brilliant insights, but our scene partners have their own agendas. They're not our mothers. They don't exist to us make us happy. All those fuckers care about is making *themselves* happy.

For instance, when creating my Given Circumstances in the *Bosch* series, I asked myself, "Who is Bosch?"

My Imagination led me to the inspiration that, "Bosch is my priest. He can absolve me. Baptize me."

That's very useful stuff. But what happens when I ask:

What is my problem?

My problem is that Bosch *isn't* my priest. He's a cop. *Finding out the truth* is what will make him happy. He doesn't give a shit about what I need.

And if I want to win my absolution, I'm going to have to fight him for it.

☙

Champions adapt.

Our movement teacher at Yale was a man called Wesley Fata. If he had lived in Ancient Greece, sculptors would have engaged in vicious catfights over who got to have Wes as their model. He was tall, blonde, lithe and without an ounce of body fat.

Fata was not the most articulate man I ever met. Dance was his language. Occasionally, though, he'd impart his surprising wisdom to us in his incongruous New York accent. He was like Michelangelo's David with Sylvester Stallone's vocal chords.

"Stay on your animal parts," is a phrase forever etched into my memory.

Another time he said, "I hear all these people saying, 'Less is more.' That's not right! Less is less! More is more!" (He was right, too. Think about it.)

I vividly recall one particular diamond in the rough that Wesley Fata shared with us:

"Champions Adapt."

When a champion like Serena Williams finds herself behind in a match, does she stick with the same losing strategy? Hell, no. Serena adapts. She changes tactics. She'll lure her opponent to the net and hammer her with a brutal passing shot. She'll force her deep into the court and run her side-to-side, whittling away at her stamina. She'll argue a call or pause to tie her shoe in order to break her opponent's momentum. Serena Williams will do whatever it takes to win. She fights. That's what defines her as a champion.

Working Actors adapt.

Say I'm playing Amanda in the opening scene of *Private Lives*. While on my honeymoon, I spot my ex-husband, Elyot. He's going to seriously fuck me up emotionally. I have to get away from here. Immediately!

But I've got a problem.

What's my problem?

My problem is that my scene partner (my new husband, Victor) comes in with his own set of Given Circumstances. That bastard's fighting for what will make *him* happy. He likes this hotel. He's already paid for it. He doesn't intend to leave.

Well, I can't let Victor get his way. The stakes are way too high for that. *I have to fight him.*

When Victor argues back, I'm forced to adapt. *I have to change my tactics.*

And in my effort to win, I'll try pretty much anything. I'll lie. I'll pout. I'll stomp my feet. I'll flirt. I'll offer sex. I'll even try to reason with him. I'll try all these tactics and more based upon Victor's behavior.

I have to win! I have to! I'm the fucking champion in this marriage, not Victor!

As a Working Actor, it's your job to win the scene from your partner. Adapt to his behavior. Change your tactics, and fight like hell.

(Winning the scene from your partner DOES NOT mean upstaging your partner, you canned ham. It means to fight for your character's happiness. Yeah, I'm talkin' to you.)

ख़

Working Actors persist.

"To err is human, to persist in it is diabolical."

So wrote the Roman philosopher, Seneca. And he knew a thing or two about the subject. He served as an adviser to both Caligula and Nero. (Nice work if you can get it.)

In *Bosch*, I worked like a sled dog to turn the hard-nosed Bosch into my priest. I confessed to a murder I didn't commit. I lied. I cried. I flirted and I fought. In short, I adapted to whatever questions and doubts he threw at me and kept trying new tactics. I persisted.

Even when Bosch finally discovered the truth about me (that I had slept with my young daughter and had covered up my son's murder to protect her), I didn't quit. I didn't stop adapting. I persisted.

I literally *begged* Bosch to let me take the blame for my son's murder, to "wash me white as snow." And when he denied me my absolution, I went out and killed the real murderer myself. I refused to be denied my baptism.

My final line to Bosch was, "I did what you couldn't do."

See, in the end, I washed *myself* as white as snow. I won.

You will not win every scene you'll ever play. But here's my best advice: Die Trying.

※

Some people struggle against inner demons.

For instance, I once played a deranged rapist on *NYPD Blue*. In an effort to suppress my perverted desires for happiness, I vowed to stay in my room, read the Bible and drink nothing but plain water. I lost that battle.

Many of the most compelling characters ever written not only fight against those who would deny them their happiness but against themselves as well.

Entire television series have been constructed around the inner conflict of their protagonist, wherein the age-old struggle between good and evil doesn't rage between the hero and an archetypical bad guy but between the protagonist or in some cases, the antihero and himself. Think Tony Soprano—or Walter White from *Breaking Bad*.

Conflicted characters are always the most interesting to play. So, as you explore "What is my problem?," always ask what your internal conflict might be.

What if, in asking "What is my problem?" as you worked on the *Scene with No Name*, you discovered that "he" (whomever he might be) is dead?

Perhaps you, as ACTOR 1, are struggling with your grief while at the same time confronting your partner. How might that affect your behavior? What if you killed the asshole? Would that change things?

No one will know what your Given Circumstances are. Nobody will have a clue what your Imagination has created.

A lot of the stuff you come up with won't be in the script. It's secret. It's private. It's yours.

The same is true of your Preparation. No one will ever know how you self-stimulated your emotions. They won't know if you used Imaginary Circumstances or Affective Memory. And they won't care.

And even if you tried to explain it to them, "civilians" wouldn't understand a word you were saying. All they see is a Working Actor living truthfully. To them, it's magic. To you, it's just another day at the office.

☙

Fuck making "choices." When working on a part, engage your Imagination. Ask these five questions:

> **Who am I?**
>
> **Who are they?**
>
> **Who are they to me?**

What will make me happy?

What is my problem?

Then ...

Fight for your Happiness. Adapt. Change tactics. Persist. Fight to win.

CHAPTER TWELVE

Storytelling

"Stories are a communal currency of humanity."
—Tahir Shah, in *Arabian Nights*

People need to be told stories. We come out of the womb hungry for tales that will help us make some sense of the world. Parents know this better than anyone.

Every culture since the dawn of recorded time has invented its own stories in the form of creation myths.

The history of the genesis of storytelling is lost in the mists of time, but sitting around the fire and listening to fables planted the seeds from which the great civilizations and religions sprang. Once we humans developed the ability to write, stories began to pour out of us.

Starting about 2700 years ago, the Greeks figured out a way to make a buck off of this most human need. They wrote plays. Then, they sold tickets.

Today, civilians pay us Working Actors to tell them stories. They buy tickets to the movies or subscribe to Netflix. They even suffer through the commercials sandwiched in between the bits of TV drama.

Working Actors are storytellers. That's what they pay us for.

༒

So far, we've worked on a pair of bullshit scenes. It's time we apply the Working Actor principles we have discussed to an actual script.

Henrik Ibsen was the greatest playwright to come along since Shakespeare. For those of you keeping score, that's about 300 years. Whether they know it or not, every dramatic writer since has been influenced by Ibsen's work.

Ibsen cranked out 27 plays in total. In a particularly fertile stretch between 1879-1892, he penned *A Doll's House, Ghosts, An Enemy of the People, The Wild Duck, Rosmersholm, Hedda Gabler* and *The Master Builder*. Not a bad resume for a crazy-haired, son-of-a-drunk from Bum Fuck, Norway.

As a student, I caught the late, great Sir Ralph Richardson (no Line Actor, he) as Old Ekdal in *The Wild Duck* at London's National Theatre.

A businessman deep into his decrepitude, Old Ekdal entertains himself by shooting the animals the family raises—inside the house.

Almost eighty at the time, Richardson's performance as the withered aphasic was mesmerizing.

At first, I was absolutely convinced that the old boy couldn't remember his lines. Every speech was an adventure and I found myself hanging on the edge of my seat, transfixed, waiting for the scene to come apart.

It was only later that I realized that the old Master was simply *improvising the part, using the lines that Ibsen had written for him.* It was riveting stuff. It was one of the first times in my life when I recognized that I was in the presence of greatness.

And Old Ekdal is a small part. In this instance, though, it was played by a lion.

As Stanislavski said, "There are no small parts, only small actors."

Though most scholars consider *The Wild Duck* to be Ibsen's best work, *A Doll's House* is his most accessible—and most produced—play. It's definitely among the most actable of his efforts.

A Doll's House is a beautiful and tense story with vivid, needy characters. It's loaded with long, challenging two-handed scenes. If you haven't read it, do so. If you haven't ever acted in it, get a partner and let her rip. You'll not find better material for a workout, and if you can successfully tackle Ibsen, reading for "piece of shit" TV shows will be child's play.

What is *A Doll's House* about?

It isn't about anything.

But ... but ... it's one of the greatest pieces of literature in the history of dramatic writing!

The lines are just a bunch of words.

You see where I'm heading with this. We approach *A Doll's House* precisely as we did with the idiotic *Scene with No Name* and as we did with the jumbled mash-up, *Come Blow the Caretaker*.

If you're concerned about the poetry of Ibsen's words, then I suggest you take up Norwegian.

If Ibsen were alive today and bought a ticket to an American production of his play, he wouldn't have a clue whether the actors were accurately reciting his precious lines. He didn't speak English.

Look, half the time, writers don't even know what they're writing about. It's up to us to figure it out for them in the telling of the story.

For his part, Ibsen thought *A Doll's House* was just a "description of humanity."

In an 1898 speech to the Norwegian Association of Women's Rights, Ibsen said that he "must disclaim the honor of having *consciously* worked for the Women's Rights Movement," since he wrote "without any *conscious* thought of making propaganda." Of course, *subconsciously* Ibsen had written one of the greatest pieces of feminist literature in history.

Marriage and childrearing haven't evolved much in the century and a half since Ibsen wrote his play. Marriage is love and gooey baby talk. It's rife with compromises and secrets. Sometimes it suffers from bitterness and oppression.

Successful marriages labor under the twin yokes of money worries and societal pressures. They struggle against unrealistic expectations, petty grievances and outright boredom.

Ibsen recognized that marriage is, by turns, both beautiful and dreadful—especially one built upon a lie.

So, fuck Ibsen's dialogue. It's up to us to tell his story.

☙

I've been hired to play Nora in *A Doll's House*. After I recover from my gender reassignment surgery, where do I start?

I start neutral, in a place of unknowingness.

I read the script. I read it again. I read all the parts in the play aloud. I say the lines by rote.

Then, I start asking questions.

Who am I?

My name is Nora Helmer and I'm almost twenty-four years old. My husband's name is Torvald and he's fourteen years older but still very handsome. His hair is starting to turn grey, but I think it's sort of sexy. He works so hard, poor dear, at the bank, and, of course, he was so sick that time. We have three super-adorable children, ages 5, 4 and 1. Yes, I am a young mother, but I just love them so much!!! I was married on my seventeenth birthday.

Mama passed away from influenza when I was a small child. I don't even remember her, poor thing. To think, I'm the age she was when she died!! I moved straight from my Papa's house to this one after I was married. I love this old house, even though it's more than we can afford.

Ah, money!!! I hate money!!! Why must everything be about money??? I am under such pressure and it's all about money. You see, when Torvald was sick, his doctor told me if we didn't go to

Italy for his health that Torvald might die!!! What would become of the children and me, then?

So, I borrowed money from that awful Krogsdad, and I couldn't tell Torvald, of course, because he was so sick. If it came out somehow, it'd cause a terrible scandal!!

Krogsdad has some stupid job at Torvald's bank, but he used to be a lawyer until he got caught forging documents and stealing money. Oh, he's an awful little man and a criminal!!! He's forever asking for his payments!!! He made me sign a contract when he loaned me the money and wanted Papa to co-sign the papers.

Papa was dying, then, and delirious and I couldn't ask him. Then after he died, I signed with Papa's signature myself. I know I shouldn't have done it, but I don't care. We needed to go to Italy. And anyway, it's all over now because Torvald has been made President of the bank and soon, very soon, I'll be able to pay off this horrible loan and I'll be free!!!

That's my version of Nora's "Who am I?" Yours would be different, of course. However, in getting ready to take this part on, this "Who am I?" would be a great starting point.

Notice I wrote it in a more modern vernacular. That's because I'm looking for things that will help me relate to this 150-year-old woman. I'm looking for behavior. I want to bring her to *life*.

Who are they?

If I'm playing a scene with my husband or against the despicable Krogsdad, that question is answered, in part, by the "Who am I?" above. If I'm working with either of my friends, Dr. Rank or Mrs. Linde, I still have a lot of questions to ask. (We'll attack the "Who are they?" in more depth as we work on the first scene of *A Doll's House*.)

What will make me happy?

In this instance, I'm looking for something that I can fight for in every scene in the play. I don't care what the eggheads say *A Doll's House* is about, nor do I give a shit that it's considered great literature. I am Nora and I just care about my own personal dilemma.

Here's what I came up with:

I'm under a lot of stress. I'm overwhelmed by my kids and my demanding husband, and I've borrowed a bunch of money from a stinking loan shark, and I'm about to bust. I'll be so happy if I can just be free!

Freedom. That's something I can play. I can fight for my freedom in every scene in the play.

Of course, the irony is that Nora thinks that if she wins her freedom from Krogsdad's demands that she'll be free. In the end, Nora comes to the realization that it's not enough. To really be free, to achieve true happiness, she has to leave her doll's house and strike out on her own as a modern woman. That's what makes the play so timeless and universal.

I couldn't care less about all of that. I'm going to fight to win my freedom in every scene of the play, starting with the first one.

☙

The opening scene of *A Doll's House* is tricky—particularly for the actor playing Torvald.

Nora enters with a Christmas tree and armloads of packages for her family. Tomorrow is Christmas. Torvald emerges from his study and chides her for her spending habits.

This problem has been exacerbated by the funds that she owes to the loan shark, Krogsdad. Money that could have been available to the family has secretly been going to pay off the loan. It's causing friction in their marriage. There's a lie at the heart of their relationship, and Torvald doesn't know it. However, his salary is set to increase greatly. Both believe that their troubles will be behind them soon.

Who am I?

I'm Nora. I've been out shopping! It's one of my favorite things to do, but I never ever get to. Well, almost never.

I bought the most delicious little doll's cradle for Emmy, an adorable suit and toy sword for Ivar and a horse and trumpet for Bob! I've even bought Torvald new gold cufflinks!!! They were frightfully expensive but I don't care. He really needs them now that he's to be the President at the bank. He must look sharp. I know I shouldn't have done it, but I've spent all the money I was supposed to give to that Krogsdad.

God forgive me, but I hate that awful bastard!!! But I don't care about him. Not a bit. Soon, I'll pay him off and forget that I never knew him. Never mind. I'll think about it after Christmas. Oh, how I love Christmas, and this is going to be the most wonderful Christmas ever!!!

Who is Torvald?

Torvald's my husband and he's very sweet, of course, but he works so much that we hardly ever see him. The children, poor things, must think that Dr. Rank is their Papa as he's here more often than Torvald!

Sometimes, I think Torvald loves money more than he loves us. He's so much like Papa that it scares me a little. That's about to change, though. He's going to take over at the bank, and we'll be rich. He can finally relax a little.

Who is Torvald to me?

This is an easy one for me. He's my father. That casts me, the Working Actor playing Nora, as a callow teenager. Answering this question opens my Imagination to a lot of new areas to explore while I improvise. (Your answer might be very different.)

What will make me happy?

Money! Gobs and gobs of money! If I can just get Torvald to give me money then I can get that awful Krogstad off my back for a while. I'll be free to enjoy Christmas!

What's my problem?

The problem is Torvald isn't going to just give me the cash. He's very frugal and he doesn't understand where all the money's going. He thinks I just waste it. He doesn't know that I have to buy my freedom. I'll have to fight for that money.

I'll flirt. I'll dance. I'll kiss him and rub him and shake my butt at him. I'll pout. I'll tease. In short, I'll do any and all of the girly things that Torvald likes in order to get that money. I'll fire my whole feminine arsenal at him.

And I'll adapt and change my tactics based on his behavior.

Now I'm ready to improvise. Almost.

Remember, the most important moment in the Improvisation is the moment before it starts.

Answering these questions might very well be enough Preparation with which to begin the Improvisation.

I've used my Imagination to create a strong set of Given Circumstances. If I need help, I can try one of Meisner's "Magic What-If" exercises. "I just found $9,000 lying in the street!" Or I can use one of Kate McGregor-Stewart's Sentence Completion Exercises. "I feel like dancing on air when _____." So long as I'm prepared, I can begin the Improvisation.

And, yes, it's still an Improvisation.

I've begun to define the parameters of my teapot in the interest of telling Ibsen's story, but it's important that I continue to improvise the scene (using the lines as written) based upon the behavior of my scene partners. That never changes. I am water. I am fluid.

In Studio A, an excellent young actress was struggling with this scene. She was, it seemed to me, intimidated by the material. I stopped her and asked her to begin again.

"Do you have a favorite Christmas carol from when you were a kid?" I asked.

She nodded.

"It's *as-if you're 12 years old and it's Christmas Eve*. Work on your song. Take a minute or two. Then come in."

After her Preparation, she came in singing a song I'd never heard in a language I didn't recognize. I have no idea what her Preparation was, but clearly the song was very meaningful to her. Perhaps it was a hymn that her Grandmother sang to her when she was a child. The song itself was not important, but it certainly resonated for her. It changed her *behavior*. She came alive. She radiated hope. She was free to improvise.

Nora enters, humming cheerfully. She is wearing an overcoat and carrying a pile of parcels. She leaves the door open behind her, revealing an Errand Boy carrying a Christmas tree.

☙

If I'm to play Torvald, this opening scene presents a very difficult challenge. Ibsen has made it even tougher on me than he has on Nora. All I do is bitch at her about money. Practically every line I have is about money.

If I'm true to the *lines* that Ibsen has written and launch into a ten-minute lecture about the evils of spending money, I'll be doing a disservice to Ibsen's *story*. The audience will dislike my Torvald right away, and they'll want Nora to leave me before the act break. I'll murder Ibsen's play before it even starts.

I've got to get back to basics.

Remember, the lines are just words. I'm trying to tell Ibsen's story.

What am I doing before the play begins?

The lines suggest that I've been "working in the study." In fact, I spend an awful lot of time in the play "working in the study."

Well, what the hell kind of work could a banker possibly be doing at home on Christmas Eve?

The obvious answer is that I'm probably not working at all. I'm avoiding the kids.

It's *as-if I'm kicking back in my Man Cave watching the Hawaii Bowl on ESPN and draining a cold one.*

I'm about to get everything I ever dreamed of. I'm going to be richer than fucking Croesus. I'm feeling no pain. I hear my piece-of-ass wife coming into the house.

That, as you can see, is a very playable Preparation. I'm ready to improvise the first scene using whatever bullshit lines Ibsen has written for me.

But that's putting the cart before the horse.

Who am I?

I'm Torvald Helmer. I'm 38 years old. I'm a little beat up from working so many hours, but I'm still in pretty decent shape for a guy my age. I've got three little kids and the hottest wife you've ever seen. I really lucked out on that one. When she dances at parties I can see all the men watching her and wanting her, but she's mine and I can have her whenever I want to. Fuck those envious bastards. Yes, she's young and sometimes immature and she blows through cash like a drunken sailor on leave in Marseilles, but that doesn't really matter now. I'm going to be President of the bank.

It's taken me twenty years of hard work to get here. I'm going to make a bunch of damn money now, and I can do whatever the hell I want to with it. I'm going to invest in properties and travel and buy nice things for my wife. I can finally enjoy myself a little.

That's a good start. I read the play a couple of times. I let my Imagination get to work. I've created a workable set of Given Circumstances. Now, it's time to look at the opening scene.

Who am I?

I'm Torvald Helmer. I'm sitting by the fire with my feet up on the ottoman. I'm on my second glass of port. What the hell? It's

Christmas, right? I'm smoking one of those monster cigars that the Chairman gave me for Christmas. Best damn smoke I've ever had. Might have to buy me a box or two of those once the checks start pouring in. Man, this is the life. You know what would make this perfect? Some pussy.

Who is Nora?

Nora's everything I ever dreamed of in a wife. I never tire of looking at her. She's funny. She's talented. She's a pretty good mother to the kids. She's got some growing up to do, but I've got time. I almost don't even care. I'm the envy of everyone. Now that I'm to be bank President, everyone will be jealous of me.

Who is Nora to me?

I (Pat) was once in love with a woman like Nora. She was a shiny lure. Just thinking about her changes my behavior—even while sitting here at this computer.

What will make me happy?

To get laid.

What's my problem?

Problem is, even though I can have her anytime I want, that's only true in theory. I can only have her when she wants. We are married, after all. I've got to work on her. I've got to fight for it.

My Tactics in the scene: tease her, please her, caress her, drop some money on her, role play as the Naughty Teacher—whatever it takes to win.

I've formed my teapot. Now I'm ready, based upon Nora's behavior, to improvise the scene within those parameters.

The beautiful irony of this scene—one that is usually considered a throwaway—is that Torvald, the moneyman, is looking for pleasure and Nora, the "happy" wife, is after his cash. And they *both* win. She gets the money she needs to buy herself a little freedom, and he walks away with the implicit promise of a hot night later on.

It's a remarkable bit of writing whether Ibsen was aware of it or not. And, again, it has nothing at all to do with his precious dialogue. The lines are just words. Ibsen gave us a great story and if we bring *life* to it, it will resonate with modern audiences. People will recognize their own quirky marriages up on that stage. They'll come face-to-face with their own humanity.

That's the job of the Working Actor.

CHAPTER THIRTEEN

Sports Psychology

"Turning pro is a mindset. If we are struggling with fear, self-sabotage, procrastination, self-doubt, etc., the problem is, we're thinking like amateurs. Amateurs don't show up. Amateurs crap out. Amateurs let adversity defeat them.
The pro thinks differently. He shows up, he does his work, he keeps on truckin', no matter what."
—Steven Pressfield

"We have met the enemy and he is us."

"Pogo" cartoonist Walt Kelly penned that phrase in 1973 to commemorate Earth Day, but it can easily be applied to the personal lives of virtually every person on the planet.

In our day-to-day existences, we are often our own worst enemies. We let our fears, doubts, laziness and insecurities defeat us.

We beat ourselves.

Actors certainly aren't immune to negative thinking. In fact, we're extraordinarily creative in finding ways to fuck ourselves up.

First of all, nerves can eat actors alive.

Early on in my career, I won a small part in a big studio feature. One of my scenes featured a Name Actor who'd made a giant splash in a couple of monster moneymakers. A ludicrously handsome guy who could act a little (but mainly faked his way through with "intensity") he seemed well on his way to becoming a big-time movie star. Guys had certainly gotten by with less.

For whatever reason, though, he'd taken a small but pivotal supporting role in this picture. Maybe he was doing someone a favor. Who knows?

There was a rumor that this actor had worked his way out of the business somehow (it was the early '90s—use your imagination) and was being positioned by his agents for a "comeback." I have no idea if that was true.

So, we go to rehearse the scene. It's just him and me in a war room with a bunch of extras. I say something then he briefs us on the operation that we're about to undertake. He's got a five-line speech. Not too tough. I mutter my words and hand the guy a file folder—and his hands are shaking so badly that he can barely take it from me.

Now, I've struggled with nervousness before. *At auditions*. Never, ever have I had that shit happen to me on a film set. (Knock wood!) By the time I get to the sound stage, I'm always prepared both physically and mentally. I know "Who I Am," and I've convinced myself that there's no one else in the world who could possibly play this part any better than me. I'm loose. I'm happy. I'm ready to improvise.

So, this poor guy's knees are literally knocking together. I feel terrible for him. Somehow, though, he makes it through rehearsal. We go to shoot it and he's sweating and quaking, and I think he might pass the hell out. I do my best to support the guy, tell him he's doing great. He's grateful. I don't know how, but he survives it. On to the next.

(By the way, the scene made it into the movie, featuring most of his performance ... FROM THE NECK UP!)

My point? Even Name Actor, quasi-movie stars can struggle with their nerves like it's opening night of *You're a Good Man, Charlie Brown* at Dick Cheney Middle School.

However, it *is* rare, and I suggest that if you can't get past your willies any better than this guy did, then maybe you should consider a different career path.

But it's not just the jitters that get in the way of our success. More often, we Working Actors defeat ourselves in a variety of subtler and even more destructive ways.

In Studio A, we were exploring the Audition Game. We were reviewing the tape of a very striking actress with strawberry blonde hair and large aquamarine eyes. She'd given an excellent reading for the part—particularly on the second pass after I had given her a silly note. (You know, the kind of note that casting people are apt to give. "Less angry" was all I said.)

Curiously, the actress was quite down on herself and seemed surprised that everyone liked it.

While we were talking, I noticed she was presently wearing a cropped leather jacket that she hadn't worn during her reading. The role was a tough homicide detective from Queens. It would have been perfect.

"I like your jacket," I said. "Why didn't you wear it during your audition?"

"I was going to," she said, the words cascading out of her mouth. "But while I was driving over here, the Voice Inside My Head said, 'That's stupid.' I do this all the time. I prepare for auditions or for work and I'm all ready and then at the last minute, I start ripping things apart. I throw everything out of the window."

I looked back at the screen. She was wearing a plain, gray tee shirt.

Sadly, she'd obeyed the Voice Inside Her Head, and the result was that she had made herself look dull, plain even.

I suspect that she doesn't know how beautiful she is.

This is true for a lot of us—women particularly. We grow up awkwardly and when the other kids make fun of our looks, we buy into it.

Even as adults, we take the word of some eighth-grade asshole we knew a million years ago and who still lives in our heads (and probably his mother's basement) instead of simply looking in the mirror, seeing what's right in front of us and accepting the truth. Our insecurities blind us.

This lovely actress had given a terrific reading, and, if this had been an actual audition as opposed to an experimental one, someone may very well have noticed. She might have won the part.

Looking at the screen, however, it would have been very easy to miss her attractiveness and ability. A harried Casting Director might have glanced at the screen and thought, "She doesn't really look the part" and moved on.

The jacket wouldn't have gotten her part, of course. A jacket is just a jacket. But I think if she had worn the jacket, it may have changed her audition. She would have felt more confident and powerful, maybe even more attractive. It would have modified her *behavior*. It would have given her another weapon to fight with in the scene. Most importantly, it would have made it impossible for anybody to overlook her reading.

Instead, this gifted actress listened to the negative Voice Inside Her Head.

She might as well have worn a sandwich board saying, "Don't look at me. I'm not that good." She obeyed that goddamn Voice Inside Her Head that makes her freak out on the way to auditions and orders her to abandon her Skill Set and her Preparation, along with her sexy jacket, at the last minute.

༄

All Athletes hear The Voice. We all wrestle with The Voice. And we all, on occasion, lose to The Voice.

But to whom does The Voice belong? And why does that bastard say such destructive things to us?

I've got a golf crony Bruce (quite a coincidence, huh?) who, every time he hits a bad shot, can be heard exclaiming in a strange sing-song voice, "Ah, Bruce! What are you doing? Why are you swinging so fast?"

What's up with that? Who is yelling at my golf buddy, Bruce?

It is, of course, the Voice Inside His Head. In this case, though, the Voice Inside His Head is making a very public appearance, and he's as mad as hell at Bruce for hooking his brand new Titleist Pro-V1 ball into a water hazard.

Just like Bruce, we Working Actors are a tad schizophrenic. There are two of us—two selves—and they are often at war with each other.

First, there's "The Athlete."

The Athlete is the actor. The Athlete has spent years in the studio working on his game. The Athlete is solid Fundamentally. The Athlete has a highly developed Emotional Skill Set at the ready. Through years of repetition, The Athlete knows how to act. Acting lives in The Athlete's muscle memory.

Then, there's that Voice Inside Our Head. Let's call that voice, "The Critic." (Boo. Hiss.)

The Critic is a skinny wanker. He reads too much. He overthinks everything. Though the closest he's ever come to entering the actual Game is to write about it for the school paper, The Critic believes he's a fucking expert. The Critic loves to give advice. The Critic lives to tell The Athlete what to do.

Of course, The Athlete already knows what he's supposed to do.

Let's say my buddy, Bruce, is teeing up his next shot. Naturally, The Critic is steaming about the quadruple bogey Bruce just took (five on and a very ugly three-putt).

If his Critic would just get out of the way, Bruce's Athlete is perfectly capable of hitting a good drive. Bruce has played for years. He's taken some lessons. He sports a twelve handicap.

But Bruce's Critic really, really, really wants to hit a good shot, and so his Critic interferes with the natural ability of his Athlete by "helping" with the shot.

His Critic starts giving Bruce instructions.

"Maybe you should relax your grip a little. Wait, wait. Remember to bend your knees. But don't forget to shift your weight to your front foot. And hit it square. Oh, yeah, and swing easy, you idiot."

Bruce grimaces, purses his lips and, for good measure, throws a little extra effort into shifting that weight.

Bruce whacks a banana ball into the trees.

You see, Bruce's Critic doesn't trust his Athlete. Forget that his Athlete has spent years working on his game. Never mind that his Athlete, through repetition, has developed the muscle memory necessary to achieve the task. His Critic is vain. His Critic thinks he knows better.

Frustrated by the sucky shot, Bruce's Critic yells at his Athlete, "Ah, Bruce! What the hell are you doing?"

Then, Bruce tightens up and vows to *try even harder* on the next shot. And so it goes. Poor old Bruce is in for a long day on the links.

⁂

The Critic is a ruthless son-of-a-bitch. He preys on Athletes at all levels—actors included.

It was The Critic that convinced a very fine actress—while she was on the way to Studio A—that her jacket was stupid and that she didn't know what the hell she was doing.

Another time in Studio A, this kid had just made a real breakthrough in his work. I paused after the lab to give him some reinforcing praise. But the kid just wouldn't hear it.

"I was terrible," he said.

I was surprised at first. Then my curiosity got the better of me. Here I was, telling this kid to his face how well he'd done, and yet he just couldn't accept my praise. What was going on here?

"Okay. You were terrible. Why?"

"Well," he said. "I messed up the lines. Then, I didn't feel right. Then, I don't know. I was terrible."

This is The Critic at its most pernicious. The Critic overreacts to everything. The Critic is a perfectionist. The Critic doesn't know when to shut the fuck up.

I'm willing to bet that every actor knows this following sequence:

Let's say you've just finished a scene. It was good—except for that one moment that didn't go quite as well as you think it could have.

This is how The Critic torments The Athlete with this information:

1.) "You blew that line" which progresses to 2.) "You fucked up the whole scene" to 3.) "You can't act at all" to 4.) "You should quit the business" to 5.) "You have no value as a human being" to 6.) "You should just go kill yourself."

This is the kind of dreadful stuff that The Critic, if left unchecked, is capable of. The Athlete fluffs a moment, and The Critic orders him to stop acting and take a long walk off a short pier. *And all because you think you may have blown one lousy line.*

The Critic is the evil, treacherous Voice Inside Our Heads.

So, how do we put this mean ass motherfucker in his place?

❦

Timothy Gallwey was a great tennis player in the junior ranks and was later captain of the Harvard tennis team.

Based on his experience teaching the game to amateurs, he published the groundbreaking book, *The Inner Game of Tennis* in

1974. He went on to write five more books in the *Inner Game* series and has sold millions of copies.

Gallwey is also a pioneer in the field of Life Coaching. He's spent decades exploring the concept of the "Inner Game" and developing his process.

Gallwey uncovered this idea of The Critic (which he calls "Self 1") and the Athlete ("Self 2"). I've learned a lot from his concepts and have applied them to my life as a Working Actor. I think they can be of great benefit to you.

I strongly recommend that you read *The Inner Game of Tennis*. It's one of the best books for actors that I've ever read.

Here is Gallwey's Inner Game formula:

**PERFORMANCE =
(POTENTIAL) − (INTERFERENCE)** [10]

Your athletic Performance as an actor equals your Potential minus Interference.

Your Potential is defined as your ability to act in that particular moment in time based on your training, your experience and you having done your homework for the project.

Interference is the Voice Inside Your Head that makes you doubt yourself and impedes your ability to perform up to your Potential.

"Mathematically," Gallwey says, "the two ways to improve Performance are to grow Potential—and the second one is to reduce the fears and the doubt, assumptions and beliefs [Interference] that get in the way of us performing at the ability we can." [11]

Increasing your acting Potential comes from learning from your experience. Your Athlete learns by doing. The more you act, the more your Athlete will know.

Your Potential lives and breathes in your muscle memory. That means you need to increase your experience as an actor by putting in hours of work in the studio, at the theater and on sets, applying your abilities to material that will challenge you. It also means you need to do your homework for each and every part. A strong Work Ethic will increase your Potential.

Reducing the Interference presents a much higher hurdle.

How do you begin to reduce the fear, self-doubt, faulty assumptions and bogus beliefs that get in the way of your Potential?

You see, your Critic makes erroneous assumptions all the time. Your Critic assumes everyone else is more confident than you are. Your Critic believes that everyone else is more right for the part than you are. Your Critic is afraid that everyone else has an inside track to getting the part. Your Critic is sure that everyone else is "luckier" than you are.

It's all bullshit, of course. No one has his shit together. As Thoreau noted:

"Most men lead lives of quiet desperation and go to the grave with the song still in them."

Each of us is plagued by doubts and fears. If we don't learn how to tame them, they'll hound us until we're in our coffins.

The belief that someone else is more right for the part than you are is a poison that your Critic pours into your ear just before you enter the audition room. It's total bullshit. You wouldn't have been called in to read by the Casting Director if you weren't right for the part. It's just the Voice Inside Your Head getting in your way.

If someone else has the inside track to getting a part, hell, there's nothing you can do about it. Besides, casting people don't generally waste their time on sessions if someone else is already cast. Again, that's The Critic rearing its ugly head.

And luck? That's just more destructive static courtesy of the Voice Inside Your Head.

As Hall of Fame golfer Gary Player once said, "The harder you work, the luckier you get."

(We'll tackle more of this kind of negative thinking when we explore Auditions in Chapter 15, but it's essential that you work to develop strategies that will help you abandon these damaging assumptions.)

Idiotic assumptions like the ones I've described are the reason I keep attacking the universal belief that acting is an Art form.

Here's why:

When The Critic hears the word "Art," it immediately starts putting pressure on The Athlete to act "better." The Critic assumes that Art requires extra effort. The Critic believes that acting is fancy. The Critic doesn't think The Athlete is arty enough. The Critic doesn't trust that The Athlete is up to the challenge. The Critic fears The Athlete will fuck up this super important work of Art.

If you were to tell your Critic that you've won a part in a project like *A Doll's House*, it will instantly assume that it knows exactly what the play is about before the first rehearsal even starts.

Your Critic has read all kinds of erudite criticism. Your Critic has seen some "really awesome" famous person play the part. So, your

Critic thinks it knows precisely how the part should be played, and your Critic is licking its lips in anticipation of telling you all of its preconceived notions.

Basically, your Critic is a dick.

Your Critic cannot wait to torment you with a thousand different head-spinning directions. Your Critic is overflowing with "brilliant" ideas that have no greater purpose than to put your poor old Athlete into a box from which she cannot escape.

So, your Athlete starts to tense up right away. All in the name of "Art."

The reason why I had my Studio A actors spend so much time working on scenes with lines taken from different plays is because The Critic can't make any assumptions in a made-up play like *Come Blow the Caretaker*. The Critic can't get in the way. Without The Critic's "artistic" expectations to fulfill, you become free to listen and to improvise based upon the behavior of your scene partners.

With practice, your Athlete can be free to attack huge projects like *A Doll's House* without your Critic's lame assumptions and false beliefs getting in the way.

Your Athlete can tell Ibsen's beautiful story without your Critic's "helpful" planning and scheming.

If you change your approach, your Critic (along with all the fears and doubts that bastard can stir up while you're taking on a mammoth part like Nora) will be forced to take a small background role. Your Athlete will be free to play the lead.

If your Critic will simply get out of the way, your Athlete, with all of her experience, is certainly capable of mastering the part.

But The Critic is not going to give up or shut up without a struggle.

☙

So, how do you reduce the fear and self-doubt that gets in the way of your Athlete's ability to act?

Whenever I express the heretical notion that "Acting isn't an art form" to an actor, and painstakingly explain my reasoning, the last line of defense is always, "Yeah, but what about *that moment*?"

Every actor knows *that moment*.

We know what it feels like when it's all working. We're loose. We're relaxed. The scene plays out effortlessly. We're completely immersed in what we're doing.

And then, *that moment*.

We can sense the air moving through space, can feel the molecules colliding with one another. Everything is dead silent. Time. Stands. Still.

That moment doesn't come along all that often, but whenever I ask another actor about *that moment*, their eyes instantly get a faraway look as their bodies recall that sublime feeling of timelessness. The mere mention of *that moment* allows the actor to revisit that mysterious state again, however briefly.

Psychologists call it a "Peak Experience."

Musicians, artists, writers and athletes all have their own terminology for *that moment*. Drummers are heard to say that they were "in the groove." Basketball players describe being "in the zone." Tennis players say they were "unconscious" or "out of their minds" during their matches.

Baseball players on a hitting streak describe seeing pitches coming at them in slow motion. They can see the seams of the baseball as it spins towards the plate *as if time itself were slowing down.*

Mihaly Csikszentmihalyi, formerly the Head of the Psychology Department at the University of Chicago and currently Professor at Claremont Graduate University, has spent his career studying this phenomenon. In addition to having a Hungarian name that's a bugger to type and a bitch to pronounce (ME-high Chick-sin-ME-high), he's regarded by many as the world's foremost researcher in the field of positive psychology.

Csikszentmihalyi has worked for decades studying *that moment.*

Csikszentmihalyi's first studies involved several hundred "difference makers" in their fields: musicians, artists, writers, chess masters, athletes, surgeons and the like. From the results of those studies, using a common theme voiced by the various participants when describing *that moment* of immersion in their fields—"a spontaneous flow"—Csikszentmihalyi dubbed his Theory of Optimal Experience as "Flow." [12]

From Csikszentmihalyi's book *Flow, The Psychology of Optimal Experience*:

"Flow—the state in which people are so involved in an activity that nothing else seems to matter. The experience itself is so enjoyable that people will do it even at great cost, for the sheer sake of doing it." [13]

Many experiences can trigger a Flow state. New love. Food. Sex. Memories. Reading an engrossing book (like this one). Watching an involving movie or a closely contested football game.

More importantly, however, Dr. Csikszentmihalyi discovered in the course of his studies that many individuals experience Flow while engaged in goal-related activities that "could not be done without the appropriate skills." [14]

In layman's terms, Flow occurs when a person is challenged by a task and finds pleasure in possessing the tools that are required to accomplish that task.

Csikszentmihalyi said Flow is "being completely involved in an activity for its own sake. The ego falls away. Time flies. Every action, movement and thought follows inevitably from the previous one, like playing jazz. Your whole being is involved, and you're using your skills to the utmost." [15]

In a Flow state, an individual may lose track of time and forget to eat. They can lose all sense of themselves.

In a TED Talk lecture he delivered, Csikszentmihalyi quoted an unnamed composer he had studied:

"You are in an ecstatic state to such a point that you feel as though you almost don't exist. I have experienced this time and again. My hand seems devoid of myself, and I have nothing to do with what is happening. I just sit there and watch it in a state of awe and wonderment. And [the music] just flows out of itself." [16]

So, it's not just Working Actors who experience *that moment*. Lots of creative types get into that "ecstatic" groove. Legit scientists have studied this state of being "out of one's mind." Peak Experience is a real thing.

So, the obvious question is: How does this concept of Flow apply to your life as a Working Actor?

Sorry to say, but this Chapter won't offer instruction in how to Flow. (Even Csikszentmihalyi doesn't attempt to teach that.) You're not going to learn here how to reach an ecstatic state or how to achieve *that moment*. What you *will* learn is how to use some new techniques in order to—

Reduce the volume of that Voice Inside Your Head so that your Athlete will be free to act.

☙

Mihaly Csikszentmihalyi estimates that the human brain can process around 110 bits of information—sights, sounds, subtleties of thought and emotion—per second. That sounds like a hell of a lot, but, to put it in perspective, having a conversation with someone uses about half that capacity. Still, that leaves a lot of room for The Critic to blunder around sticking his pimply nose into The Athlete's business.

However, given too much stimuli, the consciousness can be filled up pretty quickly, keeping The Critic too busy to intervene.

To illustrate this, we did an experiment in Studio A:

I had an actor listen while three others described where they had eaten lunch that day and what they'd had—all of them yammering at once. Afterward, I instructed the actor to close his eyes and tell us what each had eaten.

He was fairly accurate in his descriptions of the sundry burritos and salads, however, when I asked him if he could remember what each person was wearing, he drew a blank. He didn't have a clue.

The actor had been so focused on the task of listening that he had reached the limit of his brain's ability to process information. His mind was completely concentrated on the silly job I'd assigned him. He was unable to take in anything more, such as the sartorial choices of the other actors.

Where was The Critic during this exercise?

Was he busily reminding The Athlete that he was onstage and was being watched by a room full of people? Was The Critic telling The Athlete that he looked stupid or that he was doing a crappy job?

No. Of course not. The Critic had his big fat mouth shut.

Why?

In his lecture, here's how Dr. Csikszentmihalyi described the Optimal Experience of his subject, the musical composer:

"Once you are really involved in this completely engaging process of creating something new, as this man does, he doesn't have enough attention left to monitor how his body feels or his problems at home. He can't feel even that he's hungry or tired. His body disappears. His identity disappears from his consciousness, because he doesn't have enough attention, like none of us do, to really do well [at] something that requires a lot of concentration and to feel at the same time that he exists. Existence—temporarily suspended." [17]

Immersed in his activity, the composer didn't even have enough remaining concentration to notice his bodily needs. Wow!

Likewise, at the moment of his immersion in the task I'd given him, the Working Actor's Critic disappeared, because his Critic was crowded out by the complexity of the job. His brain just didn't have the capacity to process any more information or to listen to the negative words of the Voice Inside His Head. His Athlete, on the other hand, was a very busy boy.

As Tim Gallwey suggests, one way for you to up your athletic Performance is by decreasing the Interference of your Critic that gets in the way of your Potential.

The best way to do that in your acting, I believe, is to fill up your consciousness so that there's no room left for your Critic to hinder your athletic ability.

Your goal should be to create a more immersive acting experience so that your consciousness won't have enough attention left to entertain the negative influences of your Critic. In other words, you want to—

Crowd The Critic out of the equation altogether.

If you can learn to do this, you can free yourself from the self-judgment that causes your body to tighten up during the athletic event of acting a scene. And by freeing yourself, you can perform up to your athletic ability.

Again, you're not actively seeking to reach a Flow state (although a more immersive acting environment certainly increases your odds of reaching a Peak Experience). You're simply allowing the natural ability of your Athlete to come through.

In Studio A, we paid a lot of attention to the details: the Five Questions, the Preparation and fighting to win. We worked on improvising based upon the behavior of our acting partners. We labored to break the chains of our assumptions. We immersed ourselves in activities and props and costuming. We filled up our senses with sights, sounds and smells.

Essentially, we crowded the front seat of the car with so much stuff that The Critic had to take a backseat to The Athlete who could then grab the wheel. We *consciously* trained and prepared to act— only to give up control to the *subconscious* (The Athlete) at the critical moment of the athletic event.

Essentially, we trained ourselves to relax and to trust the natural ability of The Athlete.

Relax and trust your natural ability.

So how do we "relax?"

"Remember to breathe," is a familiar refrain with acting coaches. And frankly, it sucks.

Let's cast that off.

Breathing is a natural process. If you've forgotten to breathe, then you've got a bigger problem than trying to nab a part on some "piece of shit" sitcom. You're dead. No one ever "forgets" to breathe, so why are you telling yourself to "remember" to breathe?

If I'm at an audition or preparing to work and I feel tightness starting to creep in and I start telling myself to breathe, it sets off a thermonuclear chain reaction of crazy. I become even more self-aware. It's like purposely inviting The Critic to the party.

OPENING NIGHT

(STARRING THE CRITIC)

THE CRITIC: Hey. HEY. Listen to me. You're getting nervous.

THE ATHLETE: I'm a little tight maybe.

THE CRITIC: Remember to breathe.

THE ATHLETE: I'm already breathing.

THE CRITIC: Feel that? Your heart's starting to race! Breathe!

THE ATHLETE: Ok. Ok. (Inhales.)

THE CRITIC: Your blood pressure's spiking! BREATHE, DAMN YOU!!

THE ATHLETE: (Sucking wind.)

THE CRITIC: What the fuck is the matter with you?! Don't you even know how to breathe?!! You're gonna forget all your lines, asshole!!! You should have gone to law school like Dad said!!!!

THE ATHLETE: (Passes out.)

Look, if "breathing" works for you, by all means pant and wheeze your ass off. Have at it! But I have developed a different approach.

Whenever I'm getting ready to enter the acting arena, I give my Critic a job to do.

Timothy Gallwey taught his students to focus on the seams of the tennis ball. But we're acting here. No balls. (Not the kind you want to smash with a tennis racket, at least.)

So, here are two exercises I have appropriated from the Masters:

This Strasberg exercise is very popular with my Working Actors—particularly in audition waiting rooms. Try it.

Exercise One:

Study the complexity of your hands. Look at the veins on the backs of your hands, the tendons, the marks on your skin. Look at your knuckles, your fingernails. Now, study your palms. Immerse yourself in your handprint, your joints, the sensitive tips of your fingers. Note the complexity of your thumb. Look at the folds of skin where your thumb attaches to your palm. Spend five minutes studying your wondrous hands. End of exercise.

I assume you didn't forget how to breathe while you were working on it, right? Your Critic was busy and your Athlete kept right on breathing.

Here's a second one to try. We opened every meeting of Studio A with this gem I stole (and radically adapted) from Meisner. It's another effective way to put your Critic in his place so that you can start your work.

Exercise Two:

Listen. Spend several minutes listening for cars as they pass by outside. Now, move your attention further afield. Listen three blocks from where you're sitting. Listen five miles away. Listen for sounds in places an even greater distance away. Listen to your childhood home. End of exercise.

These simple exercises, given to us by the Great Ones, give The Critic something to do besides ride your ass.

Once your Critic is fully immersed in its task, your Athlete is free to act. You are in a state of Relaxed Concentration. That is your goal.

Commit to working on these exercises for a few minutes daily. Train yourself to achieve a state of Relaxed Concentration. Learn to silence your Critic. It's not difficult to do, but it takes dedication. The more consistent you are, the easier it will get and the more effective it will be. You are developing a positive, conditioned relaxation response. You are teaching your body and your mind that each time you do one of these exercises, that it is time to relax.

Timothy Gallwey wrote, "Perhaps this is why it is said that great poetry is born in silence. Great music and art are said to arise from the quiet depths of the subconscious, and true expressions of love are said to come from a source which lies beneath words and thoughts. So it is with the greatest efforts in sports; *they come when the mind is as still as a glass lake.*" [18]

Train your mind to become as still as a glass lake.

Once you have reduced the volume of that Voice Inside Your Head, you can find stillness. Then, you're free to trust the natural ability of your Athlete.

CHAPTER FOURTEEN

Overnight Success

*"It takes 20 years to make
an overnight success."*
—Eddie Cantor

Once upon a time, I became an overnight success. You can, too. Here's a story that will illustrate how.

☙

Like baseball, acting is a team sport. To be a Working Actor you've got to make the team. To make the team, you've got to try out. Except for a very small handful of elite stars, everyone has to try out.

There's a great (perhaps apocryphal) tale about the late Shelley Winters.

Winters was nearing the end of her career, and there was a part she wanted to play in some picture. Her agent tried to work it out for her, but the Casting Director wouldn't budge. If Miss Winters wanted the part, then Miss Winters would have to audition for it. Miss Winters agreed.

On the day of the audition, she sat down at the table and made a bit of small talk. When it came time to read, she opened her enormous handbag and pulled out an Oscar. She set it on the table in front of her. Then she pulled out a second Oscar. She set that one on the table, too.

"Okay, let's read," said Miss Winters.

No word on whether she got the part. But that seems beside the point, doesn't it?

☙

Casting Directors hold the keys to the castle for the Working Actor. If you plan to cross the treacherous, crocodile-filled "Moat of Irrelevance" and start working, you need to earn some fans in the casting community.

The position of Casting Director is a relatively new one in the movie business.

Fresh out of college in the late 1940s, Marion Dougherty got hired by a friend as a Casting Assistant for the *Kraft Television Show*. Four months later, she took over the top job.

At that time, casting was considered an organizational job. The studios had actors under contract and would cast directly off of their lists—regardless of whether the actor was right for the part or not. Casting people were thought of as mere secretaries.

Marion Dougherty changed all that.

The *Kraft Television Show* was shot live in New York. Marion scoured the small theaters, looking for people who could actually act. She gave a number of legendary actors their first onscreen jobs: DeNiro, DuVall, Voight, Walken, Pacino and Hoffman to name a very few.

Years later, when the studio system finally collapsed, Marion Dougherty was in a unique position to revolutionize the way that films and television shows were cast in Hollywood. She worked for the top filmmakers of her day, and she put her stamp on a long list of classic films including *Butch Cassidy and the Sundance Kid* and *Midnight Cowboy*.

I had the excellent fortune to meet with Marion Dougherty early in my career. She was, by that time, the Senior VP of Casting for Warner Bros. I was new in town and had yet to start working as an actor full-time.

My agent had set up an interview with her. I wasn't even going to get to read. I'd have much rather gotten some material to prepare. I was and continue to be (despite the evidence to the contrary provided in these pages) uncomfortable talking about myself—a probable result of my staunch Protestant upbringing.

Also, I'd had very bad luck interviewing in the past.

Once, I sat down in front of some Casting Director, a hateful, bleary-eyed woman, who said, "I have a headache. Just talk about yourself while I shut my eyes."

Fortunately for me, I had no idea who Marion Dougherty was. I just took the appointment and showed up.

Marion occupied a large office in an old building on the Warner lot. The drapes were drawn and the room was nearly empty save for an old rolltop desk and two chairs. The room was illuminated with a single, old desk lamp. I crossed a sea of blue carpeting and settled in next to her. She was perched on an ancient, wooden swivel chair.

I was fascinated—but not with her. She was an old woman, and I didn't know her from Eve. I just liked her desk.

I had grown up in a house full of antiques, and I've always had an interest in old furniture. I asked her about it. She told me everything about that desk and showed me how it worked. There was a cool secret compartment, if I recall correctly. Five minutes later, my interview was over. I don't recall if I ever said a single thing about myself.

As I was leaving, I looked back over my shoulder. She was scrawling some notes on a 3×5 index card.

Turns out, Marion kept index cards on every actor she met and stowed them away in that desk. An agent later told me that a friend of hers, a Casting Assistant, was once given the job of weeding out the old index cards. On one particular card, she had found this written:

"Bobby DeNiro. Nice boy."

I don't know what she wrote on my card (furniture fetishist, perhaps?) but I started working regularly for Warner Bros. soon after and kept working there steadily until the day the assholes fired her.

I must admit that I shed a tear the day I heard that Marion had died. And I'm sure I wasn't the only misty-eyed actor in town. She was one-of-a-kind. A veritable Who's-Who of powerful and talented Casting Directors passed through her office as assistants, and they have carried her torch for the past couple of decades.

As I said, I was lucky I didn't know who the hell she was that day or I probably would have tried too hard and made a sycophantic "Crazy Ass Bruce" of myself.

☙

When civilians ask me, "What's it like being an actor?" (doubtlessly expecting some cool fairy tale about how the movie business works) I often reply, "It's just like your job—except that before settling in behind your desk for the day, you first have to suffer through yet another job interview, and most days you get sent home with your tail between your legs."

Auditioning ain't for pussies.

In baseball, a player who hits .300 is a superstar. If he keeps putting up those numbers for enough years, that player gets into the Hall of Fame. For every ten at-bats, that living legend slinks back into the dugout seven times as a loser. But bat .250 and you're out of the league.

In the Acting Game, the percentages are lower. For example, if you bat .100, you're kicking ass and taking names.

At that rate, if you were to go on 100 auditions in a year, that would yield 10 paychecks (plus residuals). That's some real coin. Also, with that kind of exposure, it's likely that you're being seen for all kinds of potentially game-changing projects. You're a Working Actor, and you've got a shot at parlaying that into becoming a well-known Working Actor (AKA a Star).

Of course, some auditions yield more than one job. Working Actors sometimes get called in to reprise a role on a show they've already done. There are also parts that recur on TV series. You might be fortunate enough to grab several Guest Star paychecks (plus residuals) per season if you were to land a recurring role.

Still, a 10% booking rate would make you pretty damned successful. In the Commercials Game (due, in part, to the vast numbers of actors that get seen) it's more like 5%. Still pretty damn good.

Therefore, it's a virtual lock that for most of our careers as Working Actors, we will lose more than 90% of the time.

Drama School teaches us all kinds of shit: voice and speech, movement and dance, sword fighting, how to build a nose out of putty and some crap called Laban.

We learn the history of Theatre. (Did you know that ancient Greeks wore shoes called "buskins?") We learn about iambic pentameter and the Theatre of the Absurd and Commedia del'Arte.

We even study juggling and are taught career-building mime skills. If we're lucky, along the way we *might* pick up a little something about acting.

What the school "experts" don't teach is the most vital skill we will ever need:

How to audition.

I'm very grateful to have attended not one, but two, fine schools of Higher Learning. I studied under some great teachers in both New Haven and Tallahassee. I owe my career, in good part, to their training of me.

However, I consider it larceny that neither school (in the seven years that I spent in them collectively) ever spent a single hour on auditioning. Not one fucking class.

At Yale, not only did they commit the mortal sin of not teaching us how to audition, we never even auditioned for roles in the school plays. The administration simply cast the shows based on the directors' preferences and what the teachers thought the student should be working on. It was pretty bogus.

I did 35 plays in three years. Most everything I know about acting I learned during that time. My Athlete was challenged on a daily basis.

However, aside from one or two auditions for Repertory Theatre roles for outside directors, the only audition we students gave before graduation was the one that earned us a spot in the school more than three years earlier.

For some, particularly those who had been out in the business before entering graduate school, it was not a major hindrance. My classmate John Turturro was starring in a John Patrick Shanley show at Circle in the Square within months. For others, it was a rude awakening.

I sucked at auditioning. I sucked big-time. I fell flat on my face. I had been trained to be an Artist. What the fuck was this shit? Why didn't these casting fuckers recognize my GENIUS?

I had a fancy Mid-Atlantic way of speaking, because school had helped me eliminate my Southern accent. I moved gracefully (or at least as gracefully as was possible with my general white guy sense of rhythm). I was also the best damn fencer in the whole school (and had the trophy to prove it).

Why the hell didn't the professional world just fall at my slippered feet?

It was because I sucked.

I had my head so far up my Artistic ass that I could see my Adam's apple. The Critic was a very busy young man in those days. I spent a long couple of years losing spectacularly.

I once had an audition for the Asolo Theatre from Sarasota. I had grown up nearby, and it was there that I saw my very first professional play, *Two Gentlemen of Verona*. I had the honor of being accepted to their conservatory after undergraduate school.

Appearing on that stage would have been a dream come true.

My old teacher from Florida State, John Ulmer, had become the Artistic Director of the Asolo just about the time I graduated from Yale. During my last months as an undergraduate, he had somehow briefly descended into Tallahassee from New York where he had been a top Meisner teacher at Bill Esper's Studio. After a detour to Rutgers, he had returned to Florida State to take over the conservatory in Sarasota.

John had been a great teacher, a supporter of mine, and I considered him to be a friend. He had written a personal letter to Earle Gister, with whom he was acquainted, recommending me for admittance to the Yale School of Drama.

I did my audition. (I forget what the play was.)

"Jesus Christ, Skip," John said. "What the hell are they teaching up at Yale? That was awful!"

It crushed me. Here was a guy I respected, loved even, and he had just stepped on my heart. It was, and remains, the most embarrassing moment of my professional life. And [trust me] I've suffered more than a handful of those.

I limped out of there as best I could, the biggest failure in the history of the acting business. I had wasted years of my life and a pile of my parents' money, and I had nothing to show for it—except for a big old steaming pile of suck.

I put myself back into acting class. It didn't help. I kept sucking.

I took an audition class with a New York Casting Director. I did learn one thing there ("You never know!") so that proved useful in the long haul. But in the short-term, I still sucked. I kept doing readings of new plays around town, but I was a suck-ass mess in most of them.

Then, in the course of one week, two things happened that began to turn things around.

I'd come home late from some shit waiter job. Feeling like a total loser, I cracked open a Rolling Rock and plopped down in front of the TV. It was one o'clock in the morning. The only thing on was *Tomorrow with Tom Snyder*.

This was back in the old days before late-night TV became a real business. Before Snyder (an L.A. news personality) came along, they used to shut down broadcasting after Johnny Carson and put up a mesmerizing test pattern.

Snyder had bad hair, smoked one cigarette after another and had an annoying habit of barking out in laughter at his own jokes. However, he had wide interests and could make conversation with just about anyone. That was a good thing, because, about half the time, he had just about anyone with a pulse as his guest.

This night, he had on the Head of Casting for ABC Daytime.

They had to have been scraping the bottom of the barrel to come up with that booking. Sadly, I cannot remember the man's name, because if I did, I'd send him a case of wine. In the midst of a lot of jabber, honking guffaws and swirling smoke, the Casting Guy said:

"The successful actor is the actor who gets auditions."

The guy expounded on his thesis, saying that for every actor who had gotten the audition, there were hundreds that had never made it through the door—actors who never even got a shot. The actors that had received the casting call had already beaten out hundreds of other people before they even said the first line in the audition room.

They were already winners.

I was thunderstruck. It was a complete perception shift. I wasn't a failure at all! I was a success!

Thanks to that anonymous Casting Guy, I started carrying myself differently. I felt a little more confident, because, after all, I was getting auditions. I was a successful actor.

That is how I became an overnight success.

☙

The successful actor is the actor who gets auditions.

If you're getting auditions, then I, as the never humble author of this particular set of scribbles and follower of the great Oracle (AKA the anonymous Soap Opera Casting Director of the late-night TV talk show circuit), knight you, humble reader, as a successful Working Actor, and I bestow upon you all the rights and privileges that go along with that title. You are hereby entitled to change your approach and to begin viewing yourself in a more positive light. (Feel free to swagger a bit.)

If you're not getting auditions, it's your job to start getting them. Improve your Work Ethic and your Skill Set. Up your game and get your ass out there.

☙

A few days after I'd seen the *Tomorrow* show, I got a call to go meet a Casting guy for a soap opera called (ironically) *Search for Tomorrow*.

Unless you happen to be a theoretical physicist whose job it is to actually ask questions like, "Where is tomorrow?," it might be possible to put a dictionary into a blender and come up with a better show title. It reminds me of the bar sign that reads, "Free beer tomorrow." It's kind of funny—but only the first time.

Yet, the *Tomorrow with Tom Snyder* program had gotten me thinking a bit more clearly about my personal tomorrows, and it struck me as strangely serendipitous that I was now up for a show that professed to be actively searching for tomorrow.

More importantly, I had an audition. I was a successful actor.

The Casting Guy and I chatted for a few minutes, and then he shoved a stack of pages into my hand and said, "I've got a part you're right for. Steve, the Stalker. Look it over and we'll read it."

I didn't have time to contemplate what made him think that I'd be a perfect stalker. I didn't even have time to prepare. I just read it over twice. The character was obviously a very sick dude. He seemed to be under the misapprehension that he was in love with his victim, so I decided to improvise based on that.

"Ready?" he said.

I gave the best audition I'd given up to that point in my young career.

"You know why that worked?" he asked. "Because you played him as you. That's all we want to see in auditions. What you're all about."

That's what we want to see in auditions. What you're all about.

He didn't hire me. (Hey, I never claimed that the story had a happy ending.)

Look, it happens all the time. Sometimes, you knock it out of the park and you still won't get the job. Either someone will hit it a little more squarely than you did or the producers come across someone with a slightly sexier name or a cooler haircut than yours. Sometimes, the people on the other side of the table wouldn't know talent if it bit them in the nuts. The whole damn thing can be totally arbitrary. It's just part of The Game. Get used to it.

For me, however, that week proved to be the true beginning of my career as a Working Actor, because I changed my approach. I was getting auditions. I was a successful Working Actor.

You, too, can become an overnight success. Change your approach. You're already a winner.

CHAPTER FIFTEEN

The Commandments of Auditions

> *"I have ten commandments.*
> *The first nine are, thou shalt not bore.*
> *The tenth is, thou shalt have right*
> *of final cut."*
> —Billy Wilder

You must master the Audition Game.

It is almost certain that you will spend more days auditioning for parts than you will spend playing parts. To survive—to have a long career that will keep you working until you're too old to remember the lines anymore—you must learn how to consistently win jobs.

I've been auditioning for a living for more than three decades. The following Commandments reflect the lessons I've learned.

As always, absorb what is useful and cast off what is useless.

THE XV COMMANDMENTS OF AUDITIONS

THE FIRST COMMANDMENT:

They want to see YOU.

Everything else is secondary to that. The lines, your "choices," your dramaturgical skills, your clothes, your hair, the name of your school and your fancy résumé don't mean shit if you leave your Potential outside in the waiting room. They want to see your natural athletic ability. (Your "emotional equipment," as Michael Shurtleff wrote.)

Look, Shurtleff literally wrote the book on *Audition*(s). It has sold a zillion copies.

It is not my intention to rewrite the book on auditioning or to out-Shurtleff Shurtleff. If you haven't read his book, I recommend checking it out.

But Shurtleff was a Casting Director, and, as far as I know, he never went on any auditions. The lessons he learned all came from the other side of the table. While many of his insights are certainly valuable, it is impossible to appreciate what the process is like for an actor unless one has experienced auditioning from the actor's perspective.

I've been out on thousands of auditions in my life. I've won enough jobs to earn my living. I've experienced tremendous highs and dreadful lows. I know what it takes to walk into those rooms and to come out as a success—mainly because I already know that I'm a success when I enter the room.

THE SECOND COMMANDMENT:

If you're getting to audition, you're already successful.

Remember, you've beaten out hundreds of lesser mortals to get to this point. Carry that positive energy around with you on a daily basis and, most importantly, bring it with you into the audition room. You're already a winner. People respond to winners.

THE THIRD COMMANDMENT:

It's just a game.

Hey, we're not trying to cure cancer here or end world hunger. We're just trying to win acting jobs, kids.

Auditions are games. The fun is in the playing.

In all likelihood, this audition will be the only opportunity you'll ever get to play this part. You might as well let 'er rip and enjoy yourself. Have a blast. Tear it up. This is a chance to do what you were born to do.

THE FOURTH COMMANDMENT:

An audition is not a life-and-death proposition. It's one game out of many.

When the late Dean Smith retired from coaching basketball at North Carolina, his 879 wins were the most by a coach in collegiate history. He had won two NCAA Men's Basketball Division 1 Championships. His 1982 Championship team featured both James Worthy and Michael Jordan. On top of that, he ran the cleanest program in the country year in and year out. Over 96% of his players earned their degrees—an unheard-of achievement. He was by every metric a tremendous success, both as a coach and as a human being.

But guess what?

Coach Smith lost a whopping 254 games. To top it off, the Tarheels were also beaten in the Final Four a heartbreaking nine times. Nine!

Smith once said, "If you make every game a life-and-death proposition, you're going to have problems. You'll be dead a lot."

If, as a Working Actor, you're destined to lose 90% of the time, you're going to have to find a way to incorporate those statistics into your strategy so that the weight of all those temporary defeats doesn't crush you. Otherwise, you'll be "dead" pretty much all of the time.

If you are going to have a long career, you'll need to learn to put each audition into perspective.

Look, the worst thing that can possibly happen is that you walk into the audition room as a success and leave—as a success. One audition isn't going to make or break your career any more than one stinking regular season loss will torpedo a basketball team's entire season or damage a distinguished coach's legacy.

I don't want to bullshit you, though, losing sucks. No amount of positive prattle is going to change that fact. Losing 90% of the time sucks goat wads, I don't care how old or how well-adjusted you are.

So, how do you lose 90% of the time and still come out a winner?

THE FIFTH COMMANDMENT:

Don't Aim for "Success."

When it finally dawned on me that auditioning was just a game, I experimented with all kinds of stupid tricks to make it more fun for myself.

I'd make it a contest to see how long I could stay in the audition room.

Sometimes I'd come in with a long, involved (and usually made-up) story to tell or I'd dazzle them with whatever bullshit I was reading and thinking about that week. This strategy was particularly fun for me, because (to my mind anyway), it served two purposes.

First, they wouldn't be able to forget me.

Second, if all the other actors were streaming in and out of the room like clockwork every five minutes and I stayed in there for 15, it'd make the other actors think I was kicking ass and it would distract the hell out of them. (Yes, I was a total dick!)

Other times, I would enter the waiting room and pretend to fall asleep—forcing the Casting Director to come "wake me up."

Once or twice, I would even pick out some poor writer or producer in the room and pretend that I knew him. It was hilarious to watch the helpless bastard wrack his brain trying to place me.

I DO NOT RECOMMEND EMPLOYING ANY OF THESE TACTICS.

At that time, I was experimenting with different approaches to see what might make auditioning more fun for me. But in the long run, the people who cast movies and TV shows are busy folks, and it probably isn't a great idea to waste their time as frivolously as all that.

But I learned that turning an audition into a game relaxed me. My Critic was too busy laughing to get in my way. I found it easier to achieve the state of Relaxed Concentration that I was aiming for.

You see, I had lowered the stakes.

Eventually, through trial and error, I finally figured out a way to give myself a chance to win *every single audition* I went out on (without resulting to total assholery).

I changed the stakes completely. Knowing that I wasn't going to score a TD in every game (i.e. get the job) I moved the goal posts.

Instead of making every audition about getting the part, my goal is to bring *life* to the material every time I show up.

In lieu of receiving a job offer as my lone barometer of success, if I manage to bring the scene to life, I've won.

Just another Jedi mind trick brought to you by yours truly.

As neurologist and psychologist Viktor Frankl wrote in his preface to *Man's Search for Meaning*, "Don't aim at success. The more you aim at it and make it a target, the more you are going to miss it. For success, like happiness, cannot be pursued; it must ensue." [19]

Bring your audition to life. Success will ensue.

If you accomplish what you set out to do, their response (or lack thereof) will have no bearing whatsoever on whether you have succeeded.

Admittedly, you may not always be able to bring the shit to life, but changing the stakes will give you much more control of the circumstances of the audition. It will give you power.

Auditions are power situations.

What we actors fail to understand is that we have power in the equation, too.

Just because they have the part we want to get doesn't mean that we should give them all the power.

The producers have a problem, too. They have this part that they need to cast. They need somebody good, and they're afraid of fucking it up.

TV Directors have it even worse. Most of them are hired guns brought in to work for a single episode. If they hire the wrong actor, they look like idiots and won't be brought back to do another episode. That means that they won't have the money for Rainbow's braces and, well, you get the picture. Directors have issues with The Critic, too. Don't be fooled. *There's a lot of fear on their side of the table.*

THE SIXTH COMMANDMENT:

You have power.

You can solve the casting folks' problem. You are not there to please them or to get them to like you. The people on the other side of that table are your colleagues. You are their equal. You are bringing them the winning solution to their business problem.

Many times the game is lost before our butts hit the chair. Why? Because we throw away our power.

We enter the audition room as if we're scrawny, pizza-faced teenagers, dying to be loved. While this behavior may be perfectly understandable, it doesn't inspire confidence in the producers that a trustworthy professional has entered the room, ready to solve their problem.

The need to be loved is your Critic's insecure way of fucking with your Potential. If you do what you came to do and do it well, there will be plenty of love in the room after you've finished.

Casting Directors live in fear, too.

They don't make a ton of bucks by any stretch—certainly not commensurate with the hours they put in or the stress level they endure. They go job to job just like the rest of us.

THE SEVENTH COMMANDMENT:

Give good auditions.

Always. Every single time. As we've established, the successful Working Actor is the actor who gets auditions.

To remain a successful Working Actor, you must keep getting auditions.

The Casting Director has put her reputation and her livelihood on the line by bringing you in to audition. Don't fuck her over. Be good every time, and the auditions will keep coming.

How do you give good auditions?

THE EIGHTH COMMANDMENT:

Do your homework.

For a film or TV project, you'll get your sides a day—possibly two—beforehand. That's not much time, obviously. You've got to get right to work.

Start neutral. Do not waste time learning the lines. It's unnecessary. It's not a competition to see who can memorize the best. It's safe to assume that everyone knows how to learn lines. However, it's absolutely essential that you become familiar with them—particularly if they're complicated.

Remember, *the words are meaningless*. You need to know them well enough so that they don't get in the way of your athletic ability.

Work on them first. Read them aloud. Read all the parts in the scene. Spend a half an hour on the words. By reading both parts, you can get a sense of the rhythm of the scene, and *it'll help prevent your Critic from making subconscious decisions about the material*. It will also help you get a sense of what the cues are.

Next, define the parameters of the Improvisation.

Read the character description for clues. Ask yourself questions. Write a brief "Who Am I?," "Who are they?" and "What will make me happy?" Ask, "Who are they *to me*?" and "What is my problem?" Engage your Imagination.

Then—and this is crucial—*find somebody to run the scene with you.*

Audition Coaches are expensive. If you're getting a lot of auditions, it quickly becomes cost-prohibitive.

Get an Audition Buddy.

Find someone who's in the same place in the business, another successful actor who is getting regular calls. Make it standard practice to work auditions together. It will make all the difference in the world.

Prepare. Find that first moment, the moment before the scene starts. Improvise the scene based on the behavior of your Audition Buddy. Work on it in this no-pressure environment until you feel confident and loose.

THE NINTH COMMANDMENT:

Show up early.

Being late is fucking unprofessional. There will always be traffic and nobody gives a shit about your lame-ass excuses. Casting Directors want someone they can count on.

Just as importantly, you do not want to have to rush. Stress builds up adrenaline. It increases your heart rate, pulse rate and blood pressure.

Watch professional golfers on the Sunday of a tournament. As the leader moves down the back nine towards victory, he will purposefully try to slow down his gait.

Under tremendous pressure, winners work to stay loose. Walking easily towards your audition will prevent tightness from creeping into your body.

THE TENTH COMMANDMENT:

Give your Critic a job to do.

The waiting room is a clown car full of distractions. Phones ring in the outer office. Actors pace around while mouthing the lines, wasting energy and cranking up their blood pressure.

Others seem to think that the waiting room is an excuse to throw a goddamn cocktail party. They chat and carry on, creating a nuisance. While it may help them to relax, their *concentration* is out the window. Yours will be too, if you let them affect you.

Sign up on the list and find a seat. Put the script aside. You're ready. You don't need to look at it. Trust your Athlete's natural ability.

Reduce the volume of the Voice Inside Your Head. Give your Critic a job to do.

Close your eyes. Listen to the traffic outside the building. Let your imagination roam. Listen inside your house. Listen for the ocean. Listen for sounds emanating from the Cosmos. Just listen.

Look at your beautiful hand. It contains 27 bones, 27 joints, 123 ligaments, 34 muscles and 48 nerves. Consider your thumb. It's what separates you from all the other animals. Without it, you'd have to paw at the world. Look at your nails, your skin and your pores. Take your time. Look at your whole hand. SEE it.

Do what it takes to achieve Relaxed Concentration.

(God only gave Moses Ten Commandments; however, living is easy and auditions are hard. Ergo, there are five more Commandments for Auditions.)

THE ELEVENTH COMMANDMENT:

Improvise.

Enter the room as a successful Working Actor. Greet everyone cordially, without being too familiar. Take a moment to look around the room. Get used to the environment.

When it comes time to read, take a second to see the reader. What does she look like? What is she wearing? *See* her. Find something about her that will generate the first moment of the scene.

Improvise the scene using the written text. Keep up the goddamn pace. (Slow auditions are death.)

Leave the room as a successful Working Actor.

THE TWELFTH COMMANDMENT:

If they give you direction, listen to what they have to say.

Take a moment to digest the note and, if at all possible, translate it into some actable stuff. Adjust your Preparation. Add to your Given Circumstances. Often, we actors, in our eagerness to please, will start nodding and saying, "Yes, yes" before the director has even finished talking. Directors find it annoying as hell, and it can be deadly for your chances of winning the part. It's just your needy Critic again, trying to get approval!

Make sure to really listen.

Then take a couple of moments to make the adjustments. She wouldn't be giving you notes if she didn't like your reading. (You'd be out of the room.) Take the necessary time. *Add what she told you to what you were already doing.*

THE THIRTEENTH COMMANDMENT:

Fuck 'em and forget 'em.

Once your audition is over, there's no point in wasting energy worrying about it. (And don't even *think* about sitting in your car, running the "performance" over in your head again and again.) It's done.

Fuck it.

THE FOURTEENTH COMMANDMENT:

Lose better.

In spite of your enormous ability, the odds are that you were not hired to play the part you just auditioned for. For whatever reason, you "lost."

Now what?

Twenty-eight-year-old Swiss tennis player Stanislas Wawrinka had never won a major tournament. He had never even taken a set off of Rafael Nadal in twelve matches. In 2014, he beat Nadal in five sets to win the Australian Open.

Wawrinka has this quote by Irish playwright Samuel Beckett tattooed onto his arm:

> "Ever tried. Ever failed. No matter. Try Again. Fail again. *Fail better.*"

With apologies to Misters Beckett and Wawrinka, you're a successful Working Actor who is getting auditions. *Failure is not an alternative.* However, as we've established, you're destined to lose most of the time.

No matter. Your time will come. Next time, lose better.

Lose your way to the top.

THE FIFTHTEENTH COMMANDMENT:

Celebrate your victories.

Make every day you spend on the set as a Working Actor a happy one. This is what you've worked for. Savor the moment.

Relax. Concentrate. Create. Enjoy. Get into the Flow. Dare to be brilliant.

Here Endeth the Commandments. Almost.

☙

In New York, a pal of mine was auditioning for a regional theatre gig in a rented hall. They had just done a renovation on the studio. In a fit of heroic overacting, he kicked the wall. His foot went through the brand new drywall. Then, it got stuck there. When he yanked out his leg, the entire piece of wallboard ripped off the framing and fell to the floor. Needless to say, he didn't get that part.

Moral of the story: Don't do that shit.

Don't do this other shit either:

THOU SHALT NOT *try to guess what they want.*

Work on your part and play it. You know more about it than they do. Show them you. (See FIRST COMMANDMENT.)

THOU SHALT NOT *perform the stupid stage directions.*

It's an audition. Ignore stage directions that get in the way. Performing the stage directions will not get you the part. Your Improvisation will.

THOU SHALT NOT *perform the action parts of scenes.*

You can't physically grab the reader. And miming fights, etc. looks idiotic on videotape. If you're supposed have a gun or a knife in a scene, hold a finger out there—below the frame.

The same holds true for kissing, etc. You can't (and generally won't want to) make out with the reader. Cast it off. Improvise your desire for them.

THOU SHALT NOT bring props with you.

You can immerse yourself with the normal props that you carry every day: your purse, your phone or your glasses. You can use your clothes. You can use a pencil. You can always use your script as a prop, too.

Miming props or activities can work but this can be a tricky area. Don't overdo it. Audition rooms are unnaturally sterile, and natural activities help reduce some of the weirdness of the situation. *Make sure you run anything you're going to try past your Audition Buddy before you bring it to your audition.*

A friend of mine once told me a story about an audition he went on to play a Gold Rush miner. Some guy—honest to God—showed up with a burro. A fucking burro!

THOU SHALT NOT be that guy.

(Yes, a live burro!)

THOU SHALT NOT try to show them how smart you are.

If they wanted a fucking dramaturg, they'd hire one. The Critic is one smart guy. The Athlete is the actor. Choose the actor.

THOU SHALT NOT start over unless they ask you to.

If you blow a line, keep going. If you completely fall apart, ask for the cue again and go on. I've gotten many parts after having jumbled the lines. The words aren't important. You are.

THOU SHALT NOT ask to do the scene over again.

They'll feel obliged to say, "yes," but they'll be annoyed as all hell. Then, 999,999,999 times out of a billion, you'll fuck it up worse. And then they'll *actively* hate you.

THOU SHALT NOT judge your performance at the end of your reading.

I coached a woman in Studio A who, to relieve her stress, would always laugh and roll her eyes at the end of her takes. Don't do that shit. *Never apologize.* It undercuts everything you've achieved. Own your work. Thank them and leave the room as a successful Working Actor.

THOU SHALT NOT ever throw away your power. Walk out of the room a winner.

CHAPTER SIXTEEN

Rehearsal

"If people knew how hard I worked to get my mastery, it wouldn't seem so wonderful after all."
—Michelangelo

Every take is a rehearsal. There's no such thing as a performance.

☙

Congratulations! Your hard work has paid off! You won a very cool part in some total "piece of shit." You've gone out and partied with your friends. You've done the homework. You've started neutral. You've learned your lines. You've asked your questions. You've prepared. You've shown up (early) and you're ready to improvise the part based upon the behavior of your scene partners.

But, guess what? There are also technical requirements that will define the parameters of your Improvisation.

Obviously, when we're working on a play, it's necessary that we repeat the blocking the Director has worked out for us so that we don't walk out of the lights. Any business that we've worked out in rehearsal must be repeated precisely so that the action of the play can proceed in the same exact manner every single night. We need to speak loudly enough to be heard in the cheap seats. We're all familiar with these technical parameters.

Likewise, working on film requires that the action be repeated in the same way every time. We have to hit our marks.

If we button our jackets or snarf some pizza at some point in a scene, it's necessary that we repeat that bit of business as precisely as we can in every single take. Otherwise, the various takes (which are shot from different angles) won't match up in the editing room.

Also, if we vary too much from the activities we've established, the Script Supervisor (the Den Mother whose job it is to ensure continuity) will be riding our asses all day long.

We also might end up making an Internet Dork's day should a mistake make it into the final cut. Yes, there are people with nothing better to do than to "discover" the small errors that occasionally occur in shows and films. Talk about having too much friggin' time on your hands.

And, yes, we have to get Mr. Ibsen's precious words right, as well.

Hell, even TV writers are remarkably anal about the occasional stray "uh" or "well" or "yes, but" that actors sometimes try to sneak in to make the dialogue sound like something that resembles actual speech.

Getting it right. That's what our employers want. It's what they expect. It's the Working Actor's job to provide that for them.

However, in spite of the technical demands of the scene we're shooting, it's still an Improvisation based upon the behavior of our scene partners. We work the same way. The technical requirements simply add structure to our teapots. Still, we are water. Still, we are fluid.

The Improvisation in this more structured, technical environment on the set is subtler, perhaps, but it's still an Improvisation. Even though the camera may be rolling, it's not a performance. It's always a rehearsal-in-progress.

☙

We Working Actors must have a repeatable process that can be relied upon so that we're able to Improvise in spite of these technical demands.

Acting is a funny business. Sometimes, children end up in front of the camera. Most haven't studied diddly or if they have, it's all the wrong crap. Still, occasionally you'll see a tremendously affecting performance by a kid (Haley Joel Osment in *The Sixth Sense* comes to mind).

Why is it, though, that most child stars don't continue being stars after they grow up?

Answer: They never knew how to act in the first place.

They wound up on screen because they were highly photographable and wonderfully spontaneous little people. But as they grew up they weren't, perhaps, quite so cute anymore and most, never having learned the Fundamentals nor having developed the required Emotional Skill Set to transition into becoming adult Working Actors, disappeared into obscurity.

The same can hold true for young adult actors. Youth and beauty are the currency of Hollywood. Audiences want to look at pretty people. In society, it's considered bad manners to stare at other people, but in the movies you can sit in the dark and gape all you like once you plunk your money down. For this reason, a lot of beautiful young people make their way onto the movie screen.

Though a few exceptions go on to enjoy careers that span decades (Matthew McConaughey and Julia Roberts, both excellent actors, come to mind) most don't. When their looks begin to slide, and the sparkle of their spontaneity dulls, the job offers evaporate for these once-stunning beauties.

I once read an interview with a young actress. She'd had, up to that point, enjoyed quite a bit of success in the movies. She was touting her newest picture, a departure from her earlier, more juvenile work.

The movie's director had decided to shoot her co-star's close-ups first.

"'I'm such a weirdo freak actor that I can't repeat anything, and [her co-star] has done a lot of theater, he likes to do scenes over and over.' [Not having her first reactions on camera] 'made me hysterical, at the end of the day I sat in the cellblock crying. I was just done. I was so anxious to have that experience. Looking back on it now, it still makes me crazy. I want to bang my head through the table.'"

Accustomed to relying solely on her spontaneity, she melted down under the pressure of having to work outside of her comfort zone.

Will this young Working Actor survive in the movie business past her twenties and enjoy a long career?

Time will tell, but it's safe to say that her odds would greatly increase if she were to abandon the false assumption that her struggles are caused by her being a "weirdo freak of an actor." Instead of banging her head against tables, she might consider developing a stronger Work Ethic and making some effort to increase her Potential by strengthening her Fundamentals and improving her Skill Set.

☙

Over the long haul, Working Actors cannot rely solely on their spontaneity.

We discussed this story in Studio A. A Working Actor in the group whom I've known a long time admitted that he, too, had always worked the way this actress does. Not only did he always try to "go first" while shooting a scene, he never really learned his lines "all that well" so that the scene would feel "spontaneous" to him while he was working.

Through our work together, he began to understand how limiting this approach can be.

The Working Actor has no say regarding the shot list. The director decides whose coverage is done first. The Working Actor should, thanks to his Fundamentals and Emotional Skill Set, be able to shoot his coverage first or last. In fact, the Working Actor should likely *prefer* to be shot last, so that there's more rehearsal time to play with.

As for my friend's approach to learning dialogue? Here's a cautionary fable:

THE DUDE WITH FIVE LINES

(A Made-For-Television Event)

Once upon a time, I had one of the leads in a TV movie for A&E. One day, DUDE WITH FIVE LINES shows up to do a scene. We go to rehearse the thing, and the DUDE is completely unprepared. He has, as you've surmised, five fucking lines, and he doesn't know them—not a word.

> DUDE: The Assistant Director told me on the phone that I didn't have to learn my lines.

The Director, whose job it is to "make this piece of shit," freezes. Skipper and the rest of the cast slowly back away.

> DIRECTOR: [INSERT YOUR OWN SET OF EXPLETIVES.]

> DUDE: I don't really believe in learning lines, anyway.

> DIRECTOR: [INSERT ANOTHER EVEN MORE COLORFUL SET OF EXPLETIVES.]

Then, instead of hustling up and trying to cram his words in order to save himself from further embarrassment, DUDE WITH FIVE LINES spends all his time trying to convince anyone who will listen—from the Makeup Guy to the Craft Services Gal—that he was told he didn't need to learn his lines. Of course, the Director uses the DUDE as his whipping boy for the rest of the day.

The scene is in the movie. There are some lovely shots of the back of the DUDE WITH FIVE LINES' head for him to use in his reel.

CUT TO:

Two years later, Skipper is making another picture with this same Director. Between takes, the Director turns to Skipper completely out of the blue.

> DIRECTOR: Remember that fucking guy who didn't learn his fucking lines? Could you believe that fucking guy? [EXPLETIVES GALORE.]

The Director is a CAA client. And in Hollywood, word gets around quickly. It's doubtful the DUDE ever worked again.

☙

Spontaneity is earned through hard work.

I cannot stress this enough.

The belief that "not knowing your lines all that well" will somehow make you appear "spontaneous" on screen is complete and utter horseshit. It's amateur hour.

And I'm afraid this sort of "Method" is becoming more commonplace all the time.

While working on a series recently, I received a boilerplate memo from the casting office that read:

"This show is a very tightly scheduled show with much of our shooting schedule on location. ALL actors must show up to set OFF BOOK. Obviously for many of you this need not be said but in the interest of making sure we were very clear about our process when arriving on set we needed to put it out there. There will be very little time for rehearsal and no time to learn lines on the fly."

Make a copy of that memo and tape it to your mirror. It's true of every job you'll ever get.

True spontaneity—onscreen *life*—can only be achieved in a state of Relaxed Concentration. If you're trying to learn your lines "on the fly," you'll be tense. If you haven't done your homework, you'll have no chance of getting in the Flow. And boy, will it show.

LEARN YOUR FUCKING LINES.

Believe me, showing up to do a day or a week on a movie or a TV show is not as easy as it may seem.

The starters (AKA the series regulars) are in the lineup every day. They're loose. They're in the Flow. They're having fun tossing the ball around with each other.

And who the hell are you?

You're some fucking utility infielder that the Producers hired off the street. The starters want to see if you've got any game.

When I did the TV show, *The West Wing*, my old colleague from New York, Richard Schiff, told me a couple of stories about some very accomplished Working Actors who had crashed and burned under the technical pressures of the show.

The brainchild of the brilliant and mercurial playwright, Aaron Sorkin, the dialogue was intricate and the pace was rapid-fire.

The starters (Schiff, Martin Sheen, Brad Whitford, Allison Janney and the late, great John Spencer) had their shit together. They were some of the best Working Actors to ever do TV. They let 'er rip with both barrels, and God help you if you weren't ready to shoot back.

Some folks could handle it, and some, according to Schiff, couldn't. When that second event occurred, it wasn't a pretty sight.

Working on a show like *The West Wing* can be like jumping onto a moving train. Time it wrong, and you go "splat."

That's why I'm always anal about learning my damned words, backwards and forwards. I chant them. I sing them in the shower. I study them just before I go to bed so my brain can continue to work on them while I sleep.

A movie set can be a weird and pressure-packed environment. I know that if I have my lines down, I'll feel loose. I can concentrate on the Improvisation. I can have some fun. And, in the event of any weirdness, I can trust that—if nothing else—the words will be there for me.

It should go without saying, but I'll lay down the law here:

Be on time. Know your fucking words. Do your homework. Show up ready to "rehearse." These are the minimum requirements if you want to be a Working Actor.

CHAPTER SEVENTEEN

External Interference

> *"You can always find a distraction if you're looking for one."*
> —Tom Kite

In addition to the internal Interference that The Critic tries to plague us with, there is often external Interference on movie sets. As a Working Actor, it's something you'll need to learn to cope with.

Even under the best of circumstances, there can be a buttload of distractions on sets. Swarms of worker bees buzz all over the place, tweaking lights and cameras. They fuss with wardrobe and make-up and God knows what else. There are seas of background actors doing their thing. I've worked in the freezing cold until dawn and I've shot in the desert in the middle of summer more times than I'd like to remember.

There are a million ways to lose focus when there is so much going on. It can be a real challenge to achieve Relaxed Concentration in the midst of all the craziness. But it is our job as Working Actors to cultivate peace amidst the chaos.

Occasionally, the Interference can come from our fellow Working Actors.

Once, while they were shooting my close-up in a difficult scene, my TV Star scene partner continuously spat sunflower seeds at the camera crew. He fancied himself a funny guy. He was not.

Most sets are friendly. The Stars welcome their Guest Stars and Day Players into the Game and start playing. They care about their show. They want it to be good. They want it to stay on the air. They want to keep knocking down the big money.

Mainly, though, they're Athletes. They just like to play. If they weren't Stars, most of them would be working for carfare at the Dust Bunny Theater.

I spent three months working on a picture with Sam Neill, some of it on location in San Francisco.

A New Zealander, Neill was sent to European boarding schools, and attended university in England, earning a degree in Literature. He went back to New Zealand, did a bit of screenwriting and such, before stumbling into an acting gig in a movie called *Sleeping Dogs* that his pal Roger Donaldson put together.

Next came *My Brilliant Career*, and, cutting to the chase, Sam Neill became an international film and television star. In 1993 alone, he starred in both *Jurassic Park* and *The Piano*. He's a modern version of James Mason.

He's also one of the nicest men you'll ever meet.

Sam hung out with the guys. He took us all out for dinner. He showed up at my weekly poker game once or twice. He even invited a few of us over to his house in Beverly Hills for a cookout with his wife and family.

I can report that some movie stars actually grill their own burgers.

One time, I said to him, "Sam, you're a big fucking movie star, you got houses all over the globe and you're ridiculously handsome. How'd you get to be such a regular guy?"

Without batting an eyelash he said, "I come from a regular country."

More guys in the Acting Game should be like Sam Neill. His kindness and humor are infectious, and it helps create a relaxed environment on the set. Everyone gets in the flow with him, and the work is better for it.

༄

A few stars are assholes.

I learned a very important lesson early on in *my* (slightly less than) brilliant career. I hesitate to recount this story here, because: a) some people will likely react as if they're five-year-olds who've just learned there's no Santa Claus; b) others will think I simply have an ax to grind (which would be beside the point even if that were true); and, c) the fucker's dead and can't defend himself.

However, as I said, I learned a hard and valuable lesson from this man. I'm grateful to have learned it early on, and I think there may be some educational value in others hearing it. So, I hope you'll bear with me a moment while I trash a legend.

Andy Griffith was born in Mount Airy, North Carolina and graduated from UNC at Chapel Hill in 1949. Originally, he planned on studying to become a preacher but ended up taking a music degree.

In 1955, he made a Broadway splash in *No Time for Sergeants* and earned a Tony nomination. His movie debut came in 1957 with the brilliant *A Face in the Crowd*, opposite Patricia Neal, Walter Matthau and Lee Remick.

Written by Budd Schulberg (*On the Waterfront*) and directed by Elia Kazan, *A Face in the Crowd* was a perfect showcase for Griffith's prodigious musical and acting talents.

Griffith's character, Lonesome Rhoads, is a drunken bum who gets discovered by a radio producer (Neal) while he picks at his guitar in a jail cell. Intrigued, she not only puts him on the air but later takes him into her bed, as well. His homespun humor and musical prowess make him an instant hit on the airwaves and help launch him as a major TV personality.

As Rhoads' popularity grows, so does his megalomania. He goes power-crazy (Rush Limbaugh-style.) He ditches Neal for a seventeen-year-old drum majorette (Remick). Without Neal's guiding presence, his life spins out of control. His hubris finally brings about a very public downfall.

It's a Greek Tragedy with a country music chorus. Griffith is something else in it. Neal, too. If you haven't seen it, do. It's a fantastic film.

In 1960, Griffith started his eight-year run as Sheriff Andy Taylor on *The Andy Griffith Show*.

It was one of the best TV shows in history (even if it's not a great work of Art). I, like so many kids, watched it over and over in syndication. I loved the guy. Everyone did.

So, I was thrilled when I got cast in *Matlock* in 1988.

It was my third job in Hollywood. Of course, any job I got at that age brought on jump-up-and-down hysteria. I was going get to act onscreen—and they were going to pay me a lot of actual money to do it! Yippee ki-yay, bitches!!!!

And *this* job was going be extra special. It was a big, juicy part on a hit show, and (best of all) I was going get to act with one of my childhood heroes.

What could possibly go wrong?

I was recently leafing through a dictionary and I found the following definition (with my jazzy, black & white, 1988 headshot next to it):

Greenhorn, n. 1. An inexperienced or immature person, especially one who is easily deceived. 2. A newcomer, especially one who is unfamiliar with the ways of a place or group.

The shoe fit. Yes, I'd been to Yale and I'd lived in New York City. I was married. I'd produced a hit play. I had some skills. And I had a bit of swagger.

However, in terms of the movie business, I'm not ashamed to admit that I was raw. I'd done one movie, a TV pilot and a single episode of a total "piece of shit" TV show called *Houston Knights*.

At heart, I was just some dork from the Deep South.

My grandmother on my father's side was called Margaret Ray Patterson and her mother was named Maggie Durham (as in Durham, North Carolina).

My great-grandfather, J.W. Patterson, was a Carolina businessman and politician with deep roots in the state. His people came from Mount Airy—Andy Griffith's hometown, the town upon which the fictional Mayberry was based.

It seems silly in retrospect, but when I met Andy Griffith, I thought he might be interested to know about our shared histories.

I gushed a bit, perhaps, about what an honor it was to have the opportunity to work with him. Then, I prattled some shit about Mount Airy and my Great-Granny.

As the words came tumbling out of my mouth, I instantly realized that I'd made a terrible mistake, because the man staring back at me wasn't Andy of Mayberry.

It was the face of Lonesome Rhoads.

I could see myself through his eyes: as green as a sapling and dumber than tree bark. I was playing a country boy from the holler and was costumed in greasy jeans and a sweaty cap. He took one look at me and made me for a hick.

I saw a dark cloud pass over his visage as Griffith made a decision about me. He didn't like the cut of my jib, and he resolved, then and there, to teach me a thing or two about the movie business.

"Beloved" Andy proceeded to fuck with me in every imaginable way over the next couple of weeks. He whispered about me to the director and gave me acting notes and tried to get my lines cut and frowned and shook his head and wandered off muttering after my takes. He even yelled at me once or twice.

But Ol' Andy made one mistake in his dealings with me.

Truth be told, I *was* young and I *was* green and, as the descendent of hard-working cattle ranchers from the south, I certainly had generations of figurative shit on my shoes.

That said (and as a wily southern boy himself, he should have known this), being a hick doesn't necessarily mean that one is stupid.

I figured out what he was up to right away, and I decided not to let it affect me. I listened to what he had to say and if it had any value, I'd use it. Mostly, I'd just thank him for his insights and move on.

Eventually, it got so ridiculous that I just started Eddie Haskell-ing the poor guy to death. ("You look especially nice today, Mrs. Cleaver.") I'd say things like, "Thank you so much, Mr. Griffith. It's so kind of you to take such a big interest in my career!"

As he was operating under the assumption that I was an inbred bumpkin, he could never really be certain whether I was genuinely moronic or whether I was yanking his chain.

It wasn't just me either. I saw him have a go at a couple of the other Guest Stars, as well.

Once (and I consider this to be a Cardinal Sin) I even saw him pitch a total, screaming hissy fit at some lowly, 300-buck-a-week Production Assistant.

It remains a total mystery to me how a man with so much ability, a man who had achieved so much and who was so universally adored could possibly have been so insecure and mean-spirited.

I suppose it's possible that I caught him on a bad week. Each of us has troubles in our private lives that can sometimes affect our work. He certainly had his fair share. His son, Andy Jr., tragically drank himself to death at any early age in 1996.

Apparently, Griffith was able to maintain long-term friendships with several of his *Andy Griffith Show* co-stars, including Don Knotts and Ron Howard. A friend of mine did 55 episodes of *Matlock*, and I've heard him speak well of the man.

But once, when asked about his off-camera relationship with his *Andy Griffith Show* co-star, Frances Bavier, Griffith said, "There was just something about me she did not like."

Make that two of us, Sheriff Andy. Me and Aunt Bee.

After shooting the show, I felt pretty good about it. I had been able to stand toe-to-toe with a legendary actor, and, despite all his issues, I had held my own.

After I shot my last scene, I was able to *genuinely* thank Andy Griffith for all that he had taught me. In spite of his Interference, I'd learned a thing or two about my acting, and I had learned that I had the resiliency to do my work even under extreme pressure. I also learned how NOT to treat other people on movie sets.

The Roman Emperor Marcus Aurelias wrote:

"The best revenge is to be unlike him who performed the injury."

Finally, the most valuable thing I learned from Andy Griffith (and here's the moral of the story for you) is that no matter how many times you've watched someone on TV, no matter how much you may have admired them or even loved them, *you do not know them.*

The image someone projects on screen is not necessarily who they are. You may have spent hours watching their work, but you have not spent even one minute in their company. *You do not know them at all.*

Maybe in some odd way, this is a testament to good acting. A talented Working Actor can make us feel as if we truly know them through the character they play.

But, don't be fooled. It's a mirage.

Never, ever come to a set expecting to create a relationship with someone you've seen in the movies. You have a job to do. Do your homework. Learn your words. Be

ready to improvise your part based upon the behavior of your acting partners—no matter who they may be.

If your fellow acting partners are friendly between takes, so much the better. It's a lot more fun that way, and the work is generally better for it. If you get to play with someone like Sam Neill or Gillian Anderson or Albert Finney or John Spencer or Henry Gibson or Candice Bergen or Titus Welliver (like I have) it's a bonus. In my travels, I have found that almost all actors are a blast to work with.

If, however, you run into someone like Andy Griffith, who has gotten to the top because his insecurities have driven him there, it's your job to keep your head down and do the work.

Bruce Lee once said:

"The word 'Superstar' is an illusion."

Lee was right about that. In my experience, stars are just Working Actors who have kept on working. They're people who face the same daily challenges and insecurities that the rest of us do.

Your job, in spite of any Inteference, is to show up ready and to let the river flow.

CHAPTER EIGHTEEN

Spooky Action at a Distance

"You are all wave particles when I close my eyes. I am no more entranced by your entanglement than a butterfly is to a bee."
—Solange Nicole

Joseph Campbell once said:

"There is something magical about films. The person you are looking at is also somewhere else at the same time. *That is the condition of the god.* If a movie actor comes into the theater, everybody turns and looks at the movie actor. He is the real hero of the occasion. He is on another plane. He is a *multiple presence.*" [20]

Because actors can appear to exist in two places at once to those of us in the audience (the Observers), we perceive them to be godlike. Indeed, we *want* our movie stars to be gods.

I understand that urge.

I grew up 100 miles from Cape Canaveral.

When I was a kid, my sister, baby brother and I used to watch the rockets launch on television and then run outside to see the first stages deploy and fall back to earth. It was an awe-inspiring sight.

I lived and breathed the space program. My parents scored me autographed pictures of the Mercury 7 astronauts, and I spent hours simply staring at them.

The astronauts were heroes on a very grand scale. They defied the Earth's gravity and risked death in order to shed glory on their country, a glory that reflected even on the likes of me—a scrawny and worthless elementary school nerd.

To my younger Observer-self, the Mercury 7 were gods.

Of course, time taught me that astronauts were, for the most part, ordinary men with extraordinary jobs. They subsided on meager military salaries and lived in dumps. They had wives and kids like other guys, and they were subject to the sameness of day-to-day bullshit just like everyone else. For many of them, being strapped into a tiny bucket at the tippy-top of a giant bomb was the highlight of their lives.

These facts in no way diminish the extraordinary courage of the Mercury 7, nor do they tarnish the special place they hold in history—either the world's or mine. They were true heroes. At the end of the day, though, they were just men.

But when I was in grade school, I needed heroes. I needed gods.

And I admit it. Part of me still worships them.

Film stars, in my experience, are like the Mercury 7. They're ordinary people with extraordinary jobs. There's nothing inherently godlike about them. They're Working Actors who got to the top, due to their Work Ethic and their Skill Sets. They look good. They're loose. Coincidence (what some people refer to as luck) has worked in their favor. However, in the final analysis, they're just Working Actors.

We, the Observers, are what make them special. We see what we want to see. We need heroes, so we see heroes. We desire sex symbols, and we create them. We need gods, so we deify actors.

Is it any wonder, then, that we Observers like to watch TV shows like *American Idol* and *The Voice*? Producers yank some random kid off of a street corner or out of a hayloft and then transform that kid into an idol—a god (as in *The Voice* of God).

And these shows are successful because we Observers desperately want to believe that a complete Nobody—maybe even us—can become an idol if only the bigwigs would simply scour the grimy city streets and rutted dirt roads thoroughly enough to find us.

So, they make Stars out of Nobodies, and we clamor to worship that Star. The producers even give us Observers a chance to "vote" so that we can feel like *we* have created that Star.

It's a bit of a con job, but these shows allow us to momentarily escape our humdrum lives and bathe in the reflected glow of our idol's "rapture of being alive."

☙

This book began as a simple question:

Is a life spent as a Working Actor a life well lived?

A few years back, I came to a crossroads in my life. I wasn't working much at that time and was, to put it mildly, feeling disenchanted with the Acting Game. I began to find myself daydreaming about several parallel careers I might have pursued had I taken different paths. For instance, I might have been a judge or a journalist or the Artistic Director of a theatre company.

But, instead of cowering in my room and wallowing in my existential sludge, I decided to get off my skinny ass and try to answer the question honestly.

I spent many hours walking and thinking, turning the question over in my mind. I read voraciously. Then, I started taking notes. The idea for a book came much later.

My investigations led me far afield. In addition to reacquainting myself with the seminal acting texts and watching movies, I read books on history, psychology and philosophy.

You see, the space program scarred me forever. Thanks to the fucking astronauts, I will never completely escape my nerdiness. (Full disclosure: I read Science books ... for fun.)

An interest in Quantum Mechanics may seem like an odd pastime for an actor, but I, like most Working Actors, often find myself with just a little too much time on my hands.

I'll leave out (most of) the supercool details, because, well, it's kind of Dork City. But without Quantum Mechanics, that expensive smartphone that your awesome agent calls you and emails you on with all your glamorous appointments and call times wouldn't be worth a dirty Beanie Baby. You'd be paying for an old-fashioned answering service that would require an actual human operator. [The dreaded but cheerfully delivered phrase, "All clear!" is forever etched onto my brainpan.] Not only that, your "home computer" would be bigger than your Prius (which also wouldn't work).

Once upon a time, this cat named Schrödinger came up with a math equation that could predict the wave function of an electron based upon the forces that are acting on it. Cutting to the chase, a series of other guys figured out how to control the flow of electrons and created the transistor. Then they realized that by moving electrons through the transistor in a low or high state (0's and 1's) they could code information and, *voila!*, they created computer language.

From a thoroughly myopic point-of-view, that has worked out well for us Working Actors, because we can wirelessly print out our audition sides at home from our 2-pound tablets (which, incidentally, can process more information than the truck-sized "supercomputers" that scientists used to create the first Hydrogen bomb in 1952).

But here's one of the many weird things about Quantum theory: scientists still don't know how it works. They just know that it does.

Back in the day even Einstein didn't get it. He ultimately made fun of these new-fangled equations because they appeared to violate his laws of Special Relativity. They seemed to suggest that Matter could move faster than the speed of light—an Einsteinian no-no.

He derisively called Quantum Theory, "Spooky action at a distance."

The first time I read that phrase, "spooky action at a distance," I laughed out loud. It has always stuck with me, and these days it echoes in my mind practically every day.

Believe me, when you get to be my age, life can get really damned spooky in a hurry.

Over the last decade or so, my father, one of my best childhood friends and two of my beloved first cousins all died of fucking cancer.

These events left me no choice but to contemplate my own personal finish line. Consequently, I am pestered by some very spooky questions.

I won't punish you with wacky ones like, "Is the universe Observer-dependent? Would it exist without humans being on Earth to observe it?" or "Are there parallel universes? And if so, are there other worlds where the people I love still exist?"

But here's one you might want to try on for size:

What exactly is "talent?" And why is it that some people have it and others don't?

The Working Actor contains more than 56,000 words. There are numerous references to hard work and Preparation and Given Circumstances and Affective Memory and Imaginary Circumstances and Action. The words Improvisation, Potential and Relaxed Concentration are scattered all over the place.

But the word "talent," like an ugly, redheaded stepchild, seldom gets any mention at all. Why is that?

Because I can't teach "talent." No one can teach "talent." Talent is the "it factor." It's "the right stuff." It's a "gift." It's "fuck-if-I-know what it is."

Acting talent is a strange, amorphous substance that some of us seem to enjoy by birthright. But clearly it's not inherited. Nor is it something that can be learned. You either got it or you ain't. It's just "spooky."

To me, it's utterly bizarre how few people can act. Most of us spend the vast majority of our absurdly short lifespans observing, interacting with and obsessing over other people. Why is it, then, that virtually none of us can convincingly portray another person?

You know what I'm talking about. Give a non-actor a TV script and ask them to act out a part. The results will be laughably wooden. It's worse than watching a fucking grade school play, because grown-ups aren't even cute to look at.

99.9999999999999999999999999999999% of us can't act to save our lives. Why?

For the same reason that so few of us have the ability to compose a symphony or paint a museum-quality landscape or kick a 50-yard field goal or perform non-Euclidean Geometry.

Who the fuck knows? Spooky action at a distance?

Lacking the necessary talent to do any of these things, the vast majority of us have to be content to be Observers. That's just the way it is, I guess.

So, here's another question for you:

What, if anything, do Working Actors contribute to society?

I once met a random guy at my children's New Year's party. (This "gala" was pretty wild stuff. They dropped the ball at nine o'clock and everybody was home by ten. Just my speed.) The guy was a lawyer. I never asked his name. (It might have been Bruce.)

Lawyer Bruce was a film nut. He saw everything that came out, dozens of movies a month.

"Mostly I just watch," Bruce told me. "But every once in a while, I find what I'm looking for: something that really gets to me, something that moves me. When I see a movie like that, I can carry around the feeling I get from it for two or three weeks."

Watching a movie has the power to put Bruce into an extended Flow state. For him, "the rapture of being alive" can literally last for days on end. And he gets all this positive feedback from simply taking the time to watch—to observe.

My therapist, the peculiarly alluring Dr. Sensible-Shoes (wearing beat up clogs and a mid-calf skirt apparently crafted out of plaid sofa upholstery), once said to me:

"For most people [the Observers] their lone act of creation comes when they give birth to their child. But creative people live in a constant state of genesis."

While I don't think this is strictly true (for many Observers garden or cook, scrapbook or play a musical instrument) the Working Actor has the unique ability to create a battalion of new people (AKA characters) by simply using her own Skill Set.

We Working Actors observe the Observers. We, as Hamlet admonished, "hold, as 'twere, the mirror up to nature, to show virtue her own feature, scorn her own image, and the very age and body of the time his form and pressure."

At our very best, we Working Actors possess the power to bring *life* to people's lives, to propel our Observers into Flow experiences, to make them feel "the rapture." I'm pretty sure that doesn't make us gods, but we definitely contribute something to our culture.

And we make lively dinner companions.

☙

I gave a movie producer pal of mine an early manuscript of *The Working Actor*. He's worked with countless movie stars.

"You and I both know," he said after reading it, "it's much better to be a Working Actor than it is to be a movie star."

Never having been a star, I cannot with certainty say that this is true. But I can surmise.

There are obvious advantages to being a star. Stars make a lot of money. Stars get choices. Stars get lots of free shit. More importantly, from the Working Actor's point of view, stars get to act all the time.

The downside of becoming a star is that it also makes one a celebrity, and, for a lot of people, celebrity proves to be a crown of thorns.

One of the first jobs I got after leaving Yale was in Carson McCullough's *The Member of the Wedding* at Berkshire Theatre Company in Massachusetts. I played the groom. My baby sister, a whirling tornado of skinny knees and big dreams, was played by a girl named Carrie Hamilton.

A talented Hollywood-raised child, Carrie had starred in a TV show called, ironically, *Fame*. Hers was an unfailingly positive presence, and everyone around her lit up in her glow. Sadly, Carrie died of cancer at an early age.

Carol Burnett was Carrie's mom. When she came to see Carrie do the show, she had to sit in the booth with the Stage Manager, because, as she put it, "If I sat in the audience, no one would watch the play. They'd all be watching me."

That is the price that Carol Burnett had to pay for her actual "fame."

We, the Observers (her many fans—and honestly, who didn't love Carol Burnett?), had spent countless hours watching her in the privacy of our living rooms.

Because we loved her and deified her, we just couldn't bring ourselves to allow her to rejoin the ranks of the Observers—even to let her to sit with us in the dark and watch her own child in a play.

It was a heck of a way to pay her back for all the joy she had given us.

And that's just a small sample of the burden the celebrity shoulders on a daily basis. Miss Burnett, who from my perspective was as genuine a star as ever lived, handled it with grace and humor (as one might expect).

Other celebs, however, have a harder time dealing with it.

They freak out, they melt down and they act out. They punch photographers and crash cars. All their bullshit gets smeared across the pages of the papers and splashed onto the virtual walls of the Internet—and that pisses them off more. So, their self-destructive inner Critic takes over, and they fuck up worse.

All of this happens because we Observers watch their work and come to believe that we know them. We adore them, deify them and we think that this gives us the right to know everything about them—whether they want us to or not.

Why so many people chase the phantom Celebrity is a mystery to me, unless, of course, they don't fully comprehend what it is that they are seeking. They falsely assume that *fame is the end game* and that once they've arrived at it, *they'll have everything they ever wanted.*

I imagine Carol Burnett might have a thing or two to tell them about that.

I never spent much time thinking about becoming a star. I just wanted to act. Guess what? I accomplished that goal.

I also never got rich. I made six-figures a handful of times, but mostly I go check-to-check, bill-to-bill. My mailbox is often jammed with residual checks. Sometimes they're for a grand, but oftentimes they're for two bucks.

I once received a payment of one cent, and—get this—they withheld the penny and cut me a check for $0.00. I considered it a brilliant cosmic joke.

From *The Love Song of J. Alfred Prufrock* by T.S. Eliot:

> "No! I am not Prince Hamlet, nor was meant to be;
> Am an attendant lord, one that will do
> To swell a progress, start a scene or two,
> Advise the prince; no doubt, an easy tool,
> Deferential, glad to be of use,
> Politic, cautious, and meticulous;
> Full of high sentence, but a bit obtuse;
> At times, indeed, almost ridiculous–
> Almost, at times, the Fool."

In my own personal drama, I'm Polonius. I've been cast as a supporting player—in my own life.

In baseball terms, my career has been that of a reserve second baseman. I've bounced from team to team. I've ridden the pine. I've hit a little bit, but I never was completely able to break through. I've never gotten that clutch hit in a meaningful game.

But I've gotten to play in the by-god Big Leagues.

☙

It may be hubris for someone like me to write a book about acting, but I do feel that I have something to offer. I've tried to be as honest as I can be about my journey as a Working Actor in the hope that my experience will be of some value to you.

In doing so, I have no doubt ruffled a few feathers. I've probably even pissed off a few people. I expect that I've opened myself up to a fair amount of criticism. There will, no doubt, be some snarky reviews on Amazon:

"Pat Skipper says that acting isn't an art form. Having seen his work, we are inclined to agree."

If my book has been useful to you, I am grateful. If not, go on to Amazon and trash it. You won't hurt my feelings. They tell me that there's no such thing as bad publicity.

Look, I'm just a guy. I grew up in a small town. Due to the strength of my desire and my Work Ethic, I've gotten to act on screen for a living.

For thirty years, I've paid my bills from my acting. I have no other job. I have no other skills.

Very recently, I started to coach actors. I have not spent years in the studio, honing my "Method." I do not pretend to have all the answers. (But I believe I know what questions to ask.)

I've enjoyed a career that lots of actors would envy, I suppose, but there are many who've done better. There are times when I've been my own worst enemy. My ego self (The Critic) has interfered with my Potential in many destructive ways. There was a time when I lived too much in my head. I fucked myself up. I choked at critical moments.

Despite all of my training, for too many years I didn't have a reliable, repeatable process. If the part suited me and the circumstances were just right, I was a very good actor. Other times, I was merely competent.

I left too much to chance.

I sometimes hear people say, "I have no regrets." In my opinion, the person who makes this claim is either a sociopath or they're totally full of shit.

I regret all sorts of things.

I regret lying to my second grade teacher. I regret calling this kid in eighth grade a "queer." I regret the time I mauled a girl's breasts when I was fifteen when she clearly didn't want me to. I regret all the mean things I've done either by commission or omission. I regret things I've said and left unsaid. I regret the friends I've lost and the time I've frittered away. I regret my lost child.

I also regret the parts I didn't get and the opportunities I've missed to grow.

Columnist Chris Erskine wrote in the L.A. Times (8/03/13):

"I've never lusted for this place, and I'd caution anyone who does, because L.A. is a house of mirrors, playing on your vanity and your greed."

I deeply regret that I spent more time worrying about my career than I did about improving my Skill Set. I regret the times when I became enamored with my own reflection in that house of mirrors. I regret that I haven't worked harder or challenged myself more. I regret my vanity. I regret my greed.

Mostly, though, I am grateful. I've gotten to do what I love to do. I've worked with a lot of fantastic people. I've traveled the world (and I've occasionally gotten to see some of the nice places).

I'm grateful to have married a kind woman. She's a true partner in every sense of the word.

I'm grateful for our children and for the scientists who make the impossible possible. If my kids had been my sole act of creation, I'd consider myself a lucky man, indeed.

The most important lesson I've learned from my family is that, while a certain amount of suffering is inevitable,

it is not necessary to sacrifice happiness at the altar of Acting—or any other "Art."

The truth is, it has been my experience that most creative people are actually pretty happy—even the starving ones.

Psychologist Mihaly Csikszentmihalyi, who has spent a lifetime studying creative minds, writes:

"I have come to the conclusion that the reigning stereotype of the tortured genius is to a large extent a myth created by Romantic ideology and supported by evidence from isolated and—one hopes—atypical historical periods. If so many American poets and playwrights committed suicide or ended up addicted to drugs and alcohol, it was not their creativity that did it, but *an artistic scene that promised much, gave few rewards, and left nine out of ten artists neglected if not ignored.*" [21]

Many of us actors *are* neglected. Most of us will be completely ignored. That's the risk we assume when we hang out our shingle that reads, *"Working Actor."*

But at the end of the day, acting is just what we do. It's not who we are.

Our "success" will not be determined by how many jobs we win or by how many parts we get to play.

Don't let your life be defined by your career. Don't rely on your acting to make you happy.

You are responsible for your own happiness.

☙

Is a life spent as an actor a life well lived?

I struggled with this question for a very long time.

While it's definitely true that we actors contribute to our society (and that's no small thing), I have to admit that ultimately I found that answer to be unsatisfying.

Judges and sports writers and Theatre producers contribute to society, too. So do carpenters and gardeners and truck drivers. In fact, I can't think of a single person in my personal sphere of Observers who doesn't contribute something to society.

So, I was stumped. I thought I might not ever find a satisfactory answer to my question.

Then, I came across this quote from George Plimpton's *Paper Lion—Confessions of a Last String Quarterback*:

"The pleasure of sport was so often the choice to indulge the cessation of time itself—the pitcher dawdling on the mound, the skier poised at the top of the mountain trail, the basketball player preparing for a foul shot, the tennis player at set point over his opponent—all savoring the moment before committing themselves to action." [22]

Eureka. I found my answer.

The answer is found in the pleasure of indulging in the cessation of time. *That moment.*

I have lived my life in pursuit of *that moment*—the "spooky" moment of timelessness that is only achievable in the flow of the athletic event. It has been a worthwhile quest. It has made my life worth living.

I wish you the best of luck in your efforts to stop.

Time.

ACKNOWLEDGMENTS

When I was just starting out, I got to spend an evening boozing it up with the late, great Maureen Stapleton. I never laughed so hard in all my life.

When she won her Oscar for *Reds*, she blurted, "I would like to thank everyone I've ever met in my entire life."

I'm not as generous as Mrs. Stapleton was. I can think of a few people who can suck it.

I would, however, like to thank anyone who ever endeavored to teach me anything, starting with my parents, Marsha and Bill, and my siblings, Jere and Ted. You've taught me much and have asked for little in return except for my love and respect, which I offer freely.

I've had some great teachers over the years. I thank you all. Though some of you are gone, you are not forgotten: John Ulmer, Ed Kaye-Martin, Clyde Grigsby, Bill Levis, Don Stowell, Earle Gister, David Hammond, Andrei Belgrader, Wesley Fata, Paul Perri and Zoe Alexander.

Thanks to my high school Drama teacher, Mary Stephens, who not only got me pointed in the right direction but also taught me how to craft a proper sentence. Any lapses in grammar are my responsibility alone.

Thank you to my friend and coach, Kate McGregor-Stewart, for your instruction and for allowing to me demonstrate how I use a couple of your techniques. It should go without saying, but you are the best.

Friends are the family we get to choose, and I've chosen well. Thanks to my many friends for all you've taught me over the years. Read Heath, H.B. Holmes and Scott Lincoln, thanks for hanging in there with me for all these decades. And to my British pen pal, David Langrish, who mentored me along for many years, I offer my deep and abiding affection.

I owe special gratitude to my friends who read the very painful early drafts of *The Working Actor* and offered encouragement and criticism: Rivki Beer, Bill Kux, John Harnagel, Matt Kimbrough, Herschel Sparber, Dan Kolsrud and Eric Wong.

My long lost pal, Peter Crombie, made a serendipitous reappearance at a critical juncture during the development of this book, and I'm deeply indebted to him for his help, encouragement and his friendship.

Thank you, Terrill Lee Lankford, for your excellent advice.

I owe special thanks to the many agents who have represented me over the years. It wasn't always a money making proposition. Also, I offer my gratitude to my friends in the casting business. It's a hard job and I appreciate your support.

Thanks, especially, to my editor and partner-in-crime, Josh Galitsky. What luck it was to find a creative theatre man who also works on books. You're a great collaborator, Josh.

The Working Actor would have completely sucked without the participation of the original actors of Studio A: Tarek Alame, Alejandra Cejudo, Leandro Dottavio, Fenix Charlotte Lazzaroni, Edward Pagac, Samantha Quan and Roy Vongtama. Thanks to each of you for lending me your talent and your Work Ethic. You taught me well. Dare to be brilliant.

The Working Actor would not exist at all if I had never met Studio A member, Laura Harman. She is my protégé, my friend, my "adopted" child and my muse. "Failure is not an alternative!"

Thank you to my children, Amy and Jack. Every day I spend with you is a glorious learning opportunity. But mostly, it's just fun.

Being married to an actor is often difficult—especially one who is preoccupied with writing a book. Thank you, Jenny, for ... everything. Words fail.

Thanks for reading my book. Tell a friend!

Email me! I promise to answer: workingactormedia@gmail.com

Check out my blog/vlog at WorkingActorMedia.com

Subscribe to the Working Actor Media youTube channel

Friend the Working Actor Media page on Facebook

Instagram: @workingactormedia

Follow me on Twitter @actormedia

Kick ass. Take names. Get the job.

ENDNOTES

1. These calculations are based on reported earnings to SAG-AFTRA. Star salaries in films are capped at $250,000 per movie, and TV star salaries are capped at $25,000 per week. (Monies received by stars above those numbers are not reported to the Union. Very few performers earn above these cap amounts, but do keep in mind the figures used for these calculations for TV/Theatrical are somewhat understated.)

2. Certain portions of star salaries are not part of these calculations.

3. Again, this does not include the handful of very fortunate stars that make over 250 grand per project.

4. Joseph Campbell with Bill Moyers, The Power of Myth. New York: Anchor Books, 1991.

5. Sanford Meisner and Dennis Longwell, Sanford Meisner on Acting. New York: A Vintage Original, 1987.

6. American Masters: Sanford Meisner: The American Theater's Best Kept Secret, directed by Nick Doob. 1990. New York: WNET Channel 13, TV.

7. "Bruce Lee–Lost Interview 1971–Re-mastered–Be Water," December 9,1971, video clip, published November 10, 2014, YouTube, https://www.youtube.com/watch?v=h4FplhrJPIE.

8. Made you look!

9. Michael Connelly, City of Bones. New York: Little, Brown and Company, 2002.

10. Timothy Gallwey, The Inner Game of Tennis. New York: Random House, 1974.

11. Assoc. for Coaching Channel. "An Association for Coaching Interview–Tim Gallwey," YouTube video, 12:11, July 4, 2012, https://www.youtube.com/watch?v=q8X0v1NgXgQ.

12. TEDx Talks. "TEDxUChicago 2011–Mihaly Csikszentmihalyi–Rules of Engagement." YouTube video, 19:13, https://www.youtube.com/watch?v=7e1xU0-h9Y8.

13. Mihaly Csikszentmihalyi, Flow, The Psychology of Optimal Experience. New York: HarperCollins e-books, October, 2009.

14. Csikszentmihalyi, Flow.

15. John Geirland, 1996. "Go With the Flow," Wired Magazine. September, Issue 4.09.

16. Csikszentmihalyi, TEDx Talk.

17. Csikszentmihalyi, TEDx Talk.

18. Gallwey, The Inner Game of Tennis.

19. Viktor Frankl, Man's Search for Meaning. New York: Washington Square, 1963.

20. Joseph Campbell with Bill Moyers, The Power of Myth.

21. Mihaly Csikszentmihalyi, Creativity. New York: HarperCollins e-books, 2009.

22. George Plimpton, Paper Lion, Confessions of a Last String Quarterback. New York: Harper & Row, 1966.

www.ingramcontent.com/pod-product-compliance
Lightning Source LLC
LaVergne TN
LVHW041612070426
835507LV00008B/198